Colonial Furniture
for
Doll Houses
&
Miniature Rooms

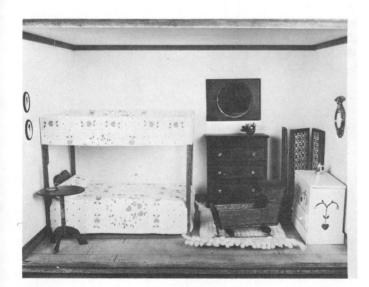

Interiors of a colonial dollhouse

Colonial Furniture
for
Doll Houses
&
Miniature Rooms

Pat Midkiff

Handcrafting miniature furniture in colonial design for dollhouses and miniature rooms.

NO POWER TOOLS NECESSARY

Pattern for miniature display room and 18 full size patterns included

Standard one-inch to one-foot scale

All patterns authentic colonial design

New England Saltbox Dollhouse

Sterling Publishing Co., Inc. New York

All the photographs in this book
are by John Read of Tampa, Florida
unless otherwise credited.

Published in 1977 by
Drake Publishers, Inc.
801 Second Avenue
New York, N.Y. 10017

Book Design: Gary Beeber

Colonial Furniture for Doll Houses & Miniature Rooms
LC: 76-27807

ISBN: 0-8473-1405-7

Printed in the United States of America

Contents

INTRODUCTION

Backward, turn backward, O Time in your flight;
Make me a child again just for tonight. --
Elizabeth A. Allen

The world of miniatures is fast becoming the pastime of thousands. Children and adults alike are making and collecting miniature furniture. Why not display your miniatures in a miniature room, add to your collected pieces some of your own, furnish a dollhouse -- there is no end to the possibilities.

I have always been interested in miniatures, art, history, and antiques, so making miniature furniture was a natural outcome. My first venture was an electrified bedroom scene with three little girls anticipating Christmas, a gift for my three nieces. Since then I never stopped: I made a dentist's office, a music room, my own colonial dollhouse, and a Shaker dollhouse with all its furniture.

After attending art school in Trenton, New Jersey and working for a short time I settled down to raise a family and pursue all kinds of hobbies: needlepoint, quilting, crewel, refinishing antiques, sewing and painting. Most of these pastimes have become subordinate to the miniatures: instead of doing them regular size I do them mini for doll-houses.

Although I've been making miniatures for years, I am always amazed by the number of requests and ideas for special orders. Many of my patterns have come about in this manner: a request for a folding screen just like my grandmother's, a spread or coverlet just like the one I had on my bed as a child. One miniature room sports an exact duplicate of the rug in my grandmother's living room, done in needlepoint. I never enter an antique shop or museum without reducing every beautiful treasure I see to the 1" -to- 1' scale -- after asking, of course, if they have any miniatures.

The scope covered by miniature collectors is never-ending. Housing for miniatures includes everything from custom-made dollhouses to regular dollhouses, miniature rooms, treasured boxes fitted with glass doors, antique clock cases, and rooms of glass. Right now I am refinishing a very old toolbox with many different compartments to house some of my own miniatures. Dollhouses range from palaces to log cabins and everything in between. They are furnished in exact period antiques of gilded gold and in cardboard pieces and things around the house. They are decorated in velvets and satins and in unbleached muslin.

When I first became interested in miniatures, I thought I was one of a very few frustrated artist-sentimentalists who still loved dolls and dollhouses, but I have come to realize that there are thousands just like me. There are three types of miniature enthusiasts -- the antique-miniature collector, the anything-small collector, and the craftsman who makes miniatures -- all with the same interest and determination. We are all microphiles -- people who appreciate the little, small, or minute -- even true micromaniacs.

A good way to keep abreast of the microworld is to subscribe to some of the magazines devoted to this field. Some of my favorites are:

Miniature Gazette
National Association of Miniature Enthusiasts
  (N. A. M. E.)
Box 2621, Brookhurst Center
Anaheim, Calif. 92801

Nutshell News
1036 Newkirk Drive
La Jolla, Calif. 92307

Mott Miniature Workshop News
1708 West Fern Drive
Fullerton, Calif. 92633

N.A.M.E. branches in many areas have annual conventions where craftsmen and dealers gather to display and sell their wares. One of the highlights of my miniature career was a convention in Boston where I first realized the enormity of the world of micro. Thousands of people came from New England, New York, Pennsylvania, and New Jersey for the two-day affair, and all had one thing in common -- miniatures. Many of my customers are from out-of-state. It's a far-reaching hobby, and hints and ideas are exchanged freely. As with any hobby, it is much more fun if you can share it with other people who enjoy and appreciate it. If there isn't a mini association in your area, start your own local group and see how fast it grows. If you have at least eight members, join N.A.M.E. and share your hobby with people across the United States. The friends you meet will be as treasured as the miniatures you collect.

Like their full-size counterparts, dollhouses and miniature rooms need interior decorating and furniture. Many shops cater to just this end; many small departments are now whole stores. Some of the many items available are: furniture, curtains, quilts, spreads, wallpaper, pictures, mirrors, dishes, food items, glassware, silver and many more. Pewter, sterling silver, wrought iron,

china, and even bread dough are some of the materials used.

Miniature collecting and crafting now rates as the second largest hobby in the United States, but in reality miniatures have been in existence since the beginning of time. The ancient Egyptians placed small replicas of a person's possessions in his tomb. Royal families gave valuable replicas of doll castles and dolls to their children. Many originals are preserved and on display in Europe. Queen Mary's dollhouse, still at Windsor Castle in England, is a popular example. The Whitney dollhouse in the United States is another beauty. It is an exact duplicate of one of the Whitney homes, furnished so exactly that it duplicates the leather-bound books in the library.

There are a multitude of books on dollhouses and miniatures; this one is written expressly to provide you with the necessary plans and instructions to join the thousands in this fascinating pastime. All of the supplies and tools needed to make the furniture described in this book are readily obtainable. One of my primary purposes is to teach the novice to become a miniaturist without a great deal of expense. It is a great pleasure to make your own miniatures and heirlooms. All patterns are included, and the simple step-by-step instructions are aimed at this goal. All the furniture shown in this book is made of balsa wood, but harder woods such as bass and cherry can also be used. If you are a neophyte in the field of furniture making, stick to balsa -- it is simple and durable, and the results are remarkable. If you are using hardwoods, more sophisticated tools are recommended: I use a small handcraft tool that has many separate attachments. All the furniture in this book can be stained in any way you desire. After you complete each piece of furniture, sign (or initial) and date it. This helps other collectors -- even your own grandchildren -- to identify it in the future. Take part in making the heirlooms of tomorrow.

IMAGINE

Imagine the feeling when you gaze at a dollhouse;
Fashioned in scale to represent years gone by.

Imagine the feelings, remembering the love;
In making the treasures that fill every room.

Imagine the feelings of preserving the past,
For future generations to relive bygone times.

Imagine

Imagine the thrill of a cherished keepsake,
Fashioned in miniature by artisans hands.

Imagine a picture, reduced to scale,
Hanging upon a dollhouse wall.

Imagine your yesterdays returned to today.

Imagine

Part I

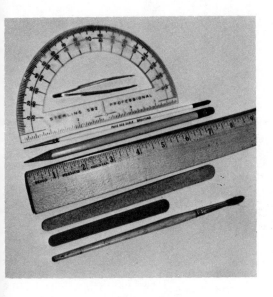

SUPPLIES AND TOOLS

The supplies and tools needed to make all the furniture in this book are as follows:

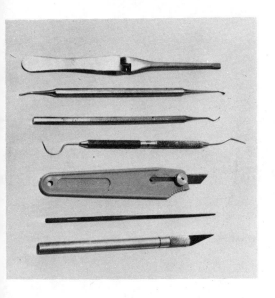

balsa wood (precut sizes are available)
    1/16" x 3" x 36"
    1/32" x 4" x 36"
    3/32" x 4" x 36"

balsa-wood strips (precut sizes are available)
    1/16" x 1/4" x 36"
    1/16" x 1/2" x 36"

square strips
    5/16" x 36"
    1/4" x 36"

dowels
    1/8" (round) x 36"
    3/16" (round) x 36"

X-Acto knife and assorted X-Acto blades
cutting board
metal-edged ruler
round craft or jeweler's file
scissors
tweezers
fine sandpaper
emery boards

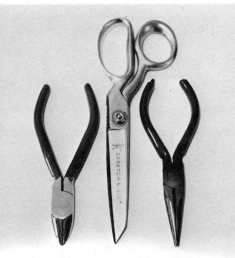

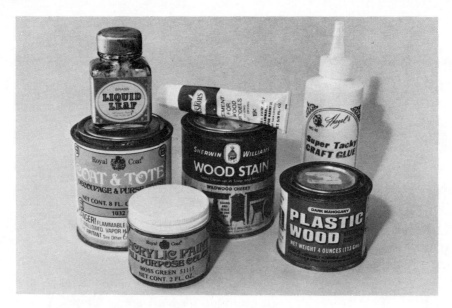

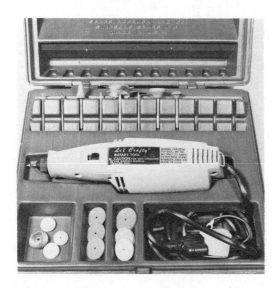

assorted small paintbrushes
heavy white craft glue
Duco cement
envelope (for storing patterns)
sheet of white paper (for mitering guide)
very sharp pencil (for tracing pattern parts)
stain
varnish or decoupage finish
needlepoint pliers
small wire cutters
paste wax (for final coat on miniature room)
small hinges (glue-on type found in craft stores)
small gold beads
framing or frame and glass (for door of miniature room)
round toothpicks
coffee stirrers (bed slats)
1/2" plywood (for miniature room)
hinges and clasp (for miniature room)
small hand tools (for hardwoods)
small jig saw (for hardwoods)

Suggested hardwoods include: basswood, fine-grain mahogany, beechwood, walnut, and maple. Any type of wood can be used if it is the proper thickness.

CONSTRUCTION HINTS

Preserving Patterns

Before tracing and cutting out the patterns in this book cut a plain sheet of white paper in half and glue two sides and the lower edge to the lower half of the inside back cover, forming a pocket.

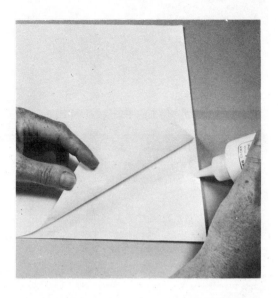

As you cut each pattern piece out of tracing paper, place it in a 3½" x 6½" envelope, label, and tuck in the back cover for future use. After you complete all the projects, add your book to your mini library.

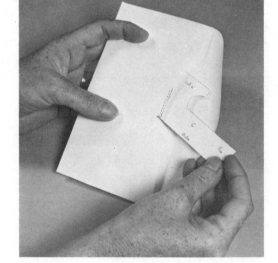

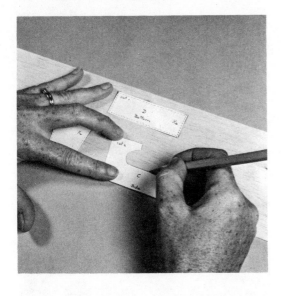

Tracing Patterns

Always trace patterns on the outside edge of the black line. You can always sand down a piece of wood to fit properly, but it is impossible to enlarge a piece. Use a very sharp pencil and as little pressure as possible to mark the wood. Balsa wood is very soft and must be worked carefully: too much pressure can crush it.

Cutting Balsa Wood

Always cut out a pattern against the grain of the wood. This prevents the wood from splitting beyond the design line. To cut against the grain, lower the position of the X-Acto knife and drag it repeatedly over the line of the cut.

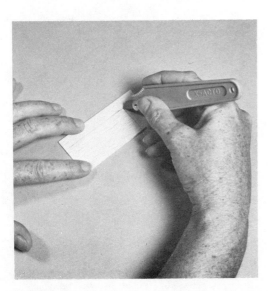

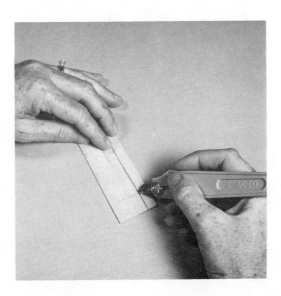

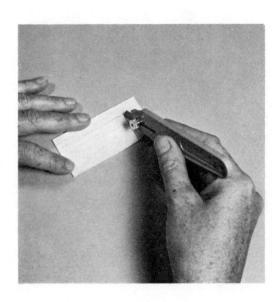

Cutting in many light strokes results in a clean, sharp edge and avoids crushing the wood. To cut with the grain of the wood, keep the X-Acto knife upright and cut a little more firmly. Always use a cutting board for balsa. I use an old bread board, but any board will do. It protects your work surface from the X-Acto knife.

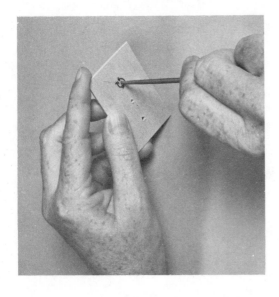

Boring Holes

I use a round jeweler's file to bore holes, but any round craft file with a pointed end will do. Place the file in the center of the spot for the hole and slowly rotate it until the hole is the desired size.

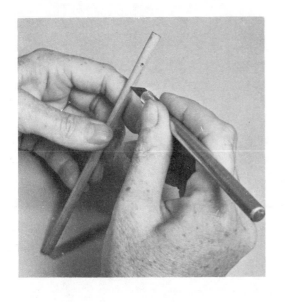

To make a hole in pieces of harder wood, such as the dowels for canopy beds or ladderback chairs, start the hole with a sharp, pointed knife and rotate. A small craft tool comes in handy.

After the hole is started, insert the round file and continue rotating until the hole is the desired size.

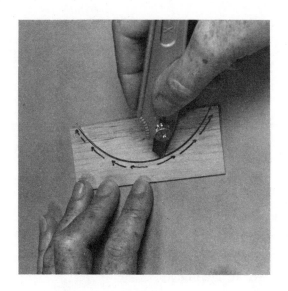

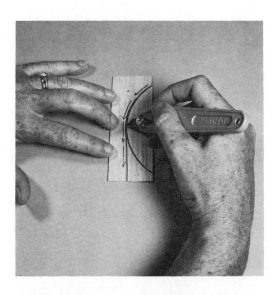

Cutting Curves

Always cut a curve from the center to prevent splitting. Cut on the outside of the cutting line to allow for sanding.

Cutting with a Ruler

To cut balsa with a ruler, balance the ruler underneath with a piece of wood the same size as that being cut. This prevents the edges from slanting.

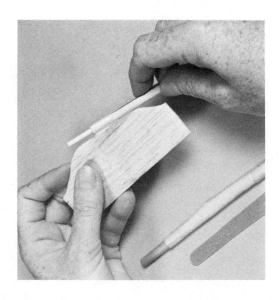

Sanding

Fine and very fine sandpaper and emery boards are sufficient for all sanding. Wrap sandpaper around a piece of doweling and tape both ends securely. Use this tool to sand curves and hard-to-reach parts. Use emery boards for straight edges.

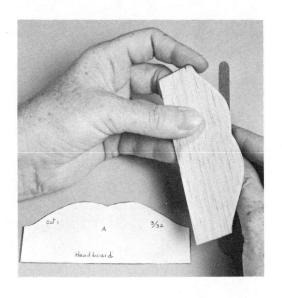

In the instructions the term "half-round" means to sand only one side, usually the outside or top of the piece. "Full-round" means to sand both sides to form a rounded edge.

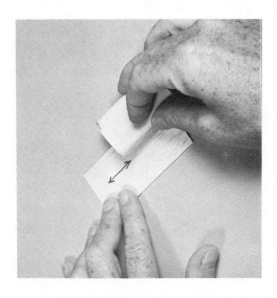

Always sand with the grain of the wood to achieve a flat surface. Circular or erratic motions mark the surface of the wood.

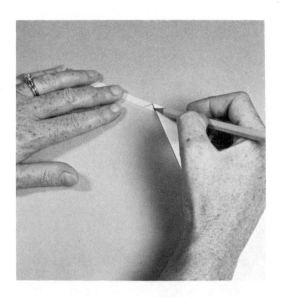

Mitering

Mitering balsa wood is easier with a piece of paper folded into a 45° angle. I use a miter box and saw, available in hobby shops, for harder woods such as basswood. The paper method, using an X-Acto knife is very accurate.

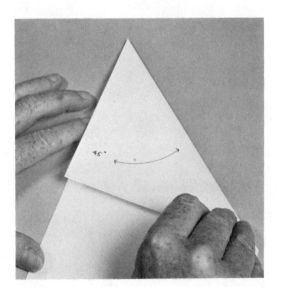

Fold the paper so that the top runs parallel to the side.

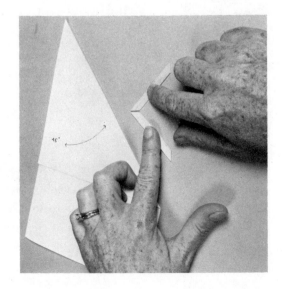

The crease represents a 45° angle. The more carefully you cut, the less sanding you have to do. Properly cut parts will fit together smoothly.

Bending Wood

To bend a piece of 1/16" balsa wood, soak it in warm water for an hour or so. Wipe excess water off with a paper towel, wrap the wood around a 32-ounce mayonnaise jar, and secure with two rubber bands. Let dry overnight.

When the wood is completely dry, trace the pattern, cut out, sand, and stain, and it is ready to assemble.

I bend large pieces of wood before I start making any of the furniture, especially slats for ladderback chairs and the cradle hood, so that I don't have to wait for the wood to dry after getting started.

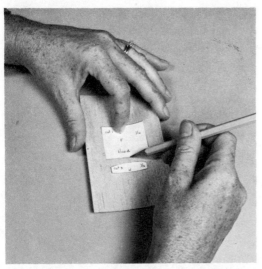

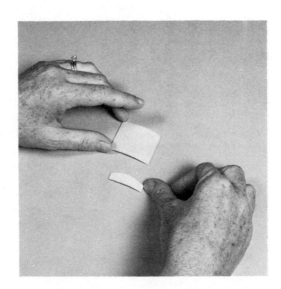

Gluing

The less glue you use, the better -- too much will leave marks. Use only enough to ensure that the pieces will hold together securely. I use thick, white craft glue that dries clear for most of the furniture. Use Duco cement for the ladderback chairs and the hinges on the tables and the top of the blanket chest.

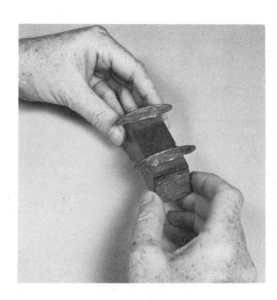

Staining

I always stain furniture pieces before I glue them together. The glue acts as a sealer and prevents the stain from penetrating the wood.

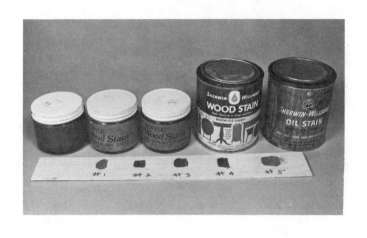

Oil-base stain penetrates balsa wood more evenly and gives a professional finish. Mix different stains to get the color you want. Use an old piece of balsa to test the color. When you get the desired shade, label and number the spot on the wood that corresponds with the label and number on the jar of stain for future use.

I combine maple, cherry, and walnut stains for my favorite color. The furniture in this book is stained with American cherry mixed with a small amount of walnut. To achieve an old look, experiment with different colors. The same piece of furniture looks quite different treated with different colors of finish.

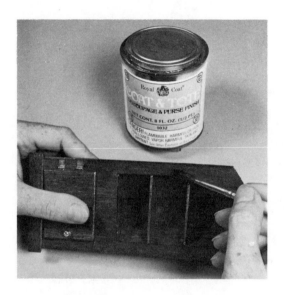

Finishing

Varnish and decoupage finishes can be used to put the final touch on your miniature furniture. I use decoupage finish. Always use two coats to strengthen balsa wood. It penetrates the wood and makes it more durable.

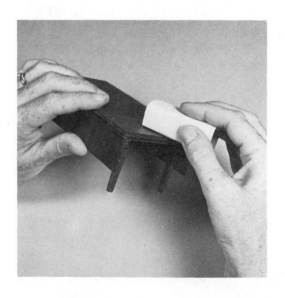

The first step is a light sanding with very fine sandpaper. Sand lightly after each coat of varnish or decoupage finish. Make sure to let each coat dry before going on to the next step. After the final coat of finish dries, rub lightly with 000-grade steel wool for a satiny shine.

Carving

Carving is accomplished by cutting away the surface
of the wood to form a design. If you are working
with balsa wood, be careful not to break the wood.
Draw the pattern on the wood and carve out the
initial design with a sharp knife. Once the design
is established, sand to achieve the final sculptured
finish.

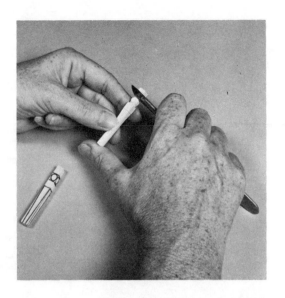

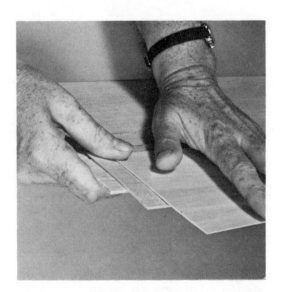

Before placing the pattern on the wood, make sure
that it is the proper thickness.

Use a small can or jar to hold your tools while you
are working. They won't be misplaced and are
always within reach.

The secret of making attractive miniature furniture is patience. Do not rush the steps -- dry glue and finishes overnight.

Experiment with your furniture. The supplies and tools are inexpensive: mistakes cost only pennies.

Be creative: design and tailor the patterns to your own taste.

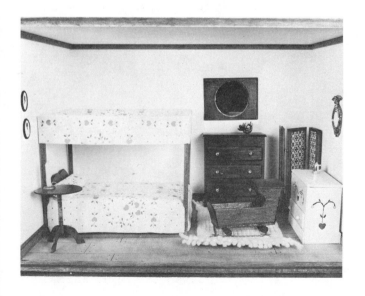

Part II

1 MINIATURE ROOM

Supplies

1/2" plywood
glass for 10" x 15" frame
1" brads
two hinges and one clasp for door

Instructions

1. Using the back (A) as a guide, nail the top (C) and the bottom (C) into place along the dotted lines with four equally spaced 1" brads.
2. Nail two sides (B) into place, using the dotted lines as guides.
3. To make the framed glass front, purchase framing and miter the corners. The outside of the frame should measure 10" x 15". Insert the glass. Many framing stores will make a frame to measure, or you can use a ready-made frame.
4. Fasten the framed glass to the assembled room with small brass hinges and a clasp.
5. Fill in nail holes with wood filler and sand smooth.
6. Sand the entire miniature room, moving with the grain of the wood. If you sand against the grain, the surface will be marred.

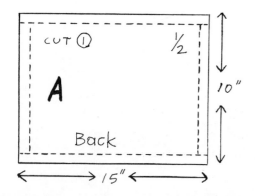

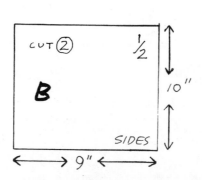

7. Stain the room the desired color.

8. After the stain is dry, varnish and let dry thoroughly.

9. After the first coat of varnish is dry, rub down the finish with 000-grade steel wool. Rub with the grain of wood.

10. Revarnish and rub down again.

11. The final step is a good coat of paste wax and a final rubbing with a soft cloth.

12. To finish the inside of the miniature room:
    a. Pencil boards in different widths to look like random-width flooring. Add dots with pencil to look like pegs.
    b. Stain, varnish, and sand the interior.
    c. Paint the ceiling.
    d. Paint or wallpaper the walls.
    e. Make baseboards with a 1/16" x 1/2" x 36" balsa strip. Paint or stain.
    f. For the ceiling molding use a 1/16" x 1/4" x 36" balsa strip. Paint or stain.

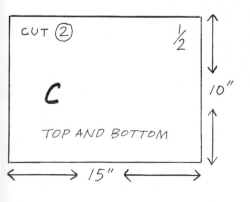

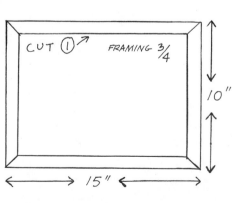

2 FIREPLACE

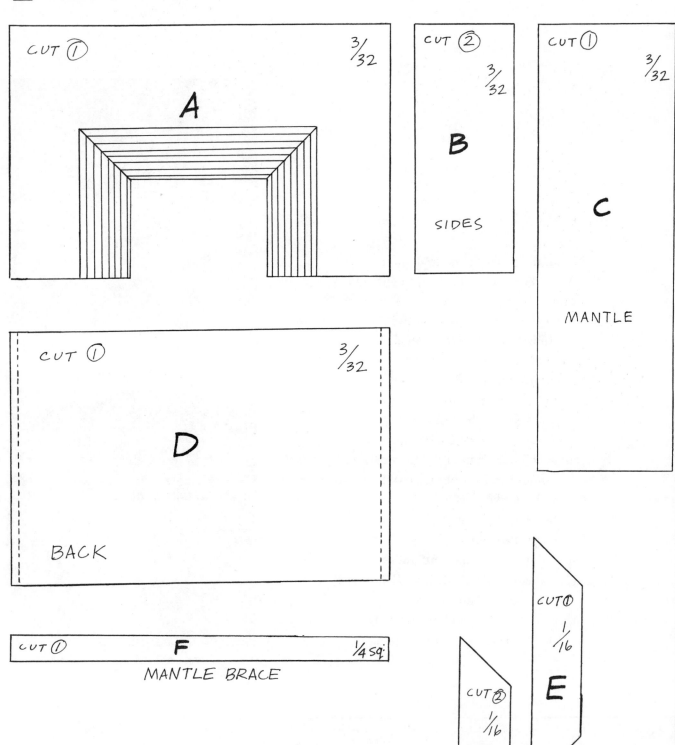

CUT ①   A   3/32

CUT ②   B   3/32   SIDES

CUT ①   C   3/32   MANTLE

CUT ①   D   3/32   BACK

CUT ①   F   ¼ sq.   MANTLE BRACE

CUT ①   E   1/16

CUT ②   E   1/16

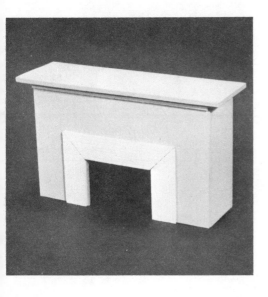

5. Join part A to two Bs.
6. Join parts C and F to the top of A, Bs, and C.

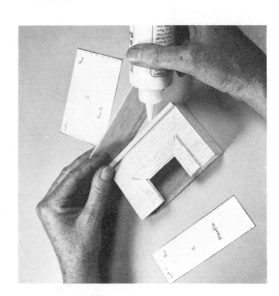

Supplies

balsa wood
   3/32" x 4" x 36"
   1/16" x 1/2" x 36"
black contact paper

Instructions

1. Cut out all pattern parts on the pattern sheet.

2. Sand all parts.

3. Make E pattern parts by drawing the back of the X-Acto knife along a ruler against the pieces.

4. Using pattern part D and the dotted line as a guide, join parts B and D.

7. Paint E parts white.
8. Paint assembled parts A, B, C, D, and F the color of the room trim.
9. Glue E parts to the front of the assembled fireplace.
10. Use black construction paper for the back front of the fireplace and for the hearth. Mark it with gray pencil to look like slates.

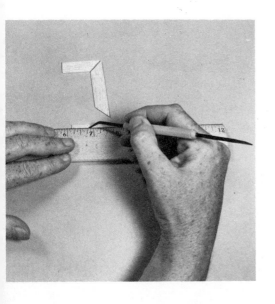

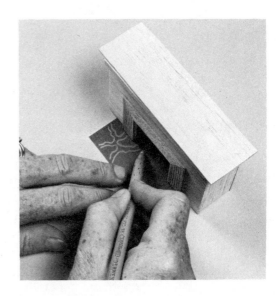

3 CHAIR & SOFA

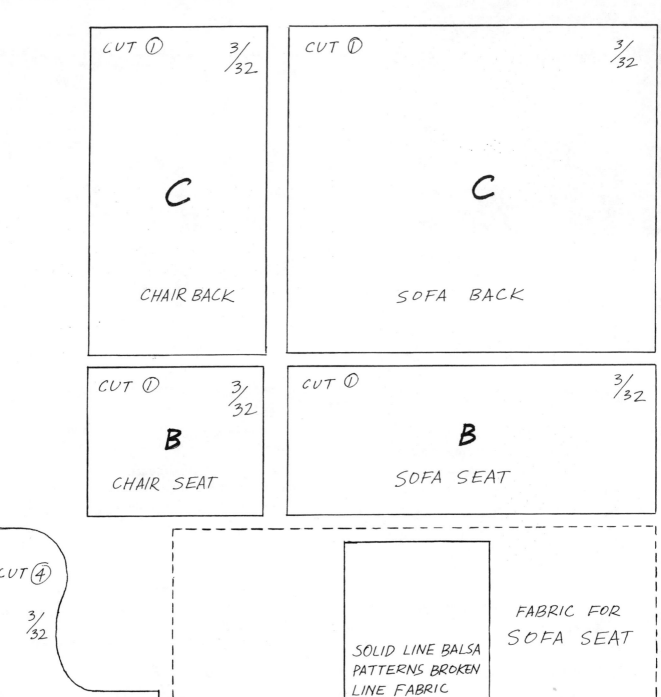

CUT ①   3/32

C

CHAIR BACK

CUT ①   3/32

C

SOFA BACK

CUT ①   3/32

B

CHAIR SEAT

CUT ①   3/32

B

SOFA SEAT

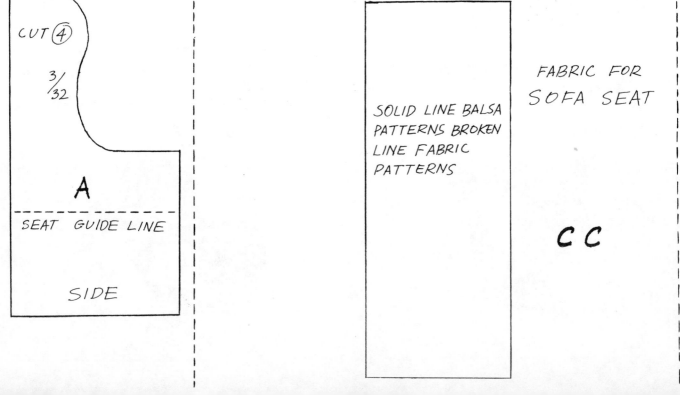

CUT ④

3/32

A

SEAT GUIDE LINE

SIDE

SOLID LINE BALSA
PATTERNS BROKEN
LINE FABRIC
PATTERNS

FABRIC FOR
SOFA SEAT

C C

Supplies

fabric
3/32" x 4" x 36"
cotton padding

Instructions

1. Cut out all pattern parts on the pattern sheet.
   Sew fabric parts BB to AA, leaving a 1/4" seam.

2. Place fabric piece AA face down on a flat surface.

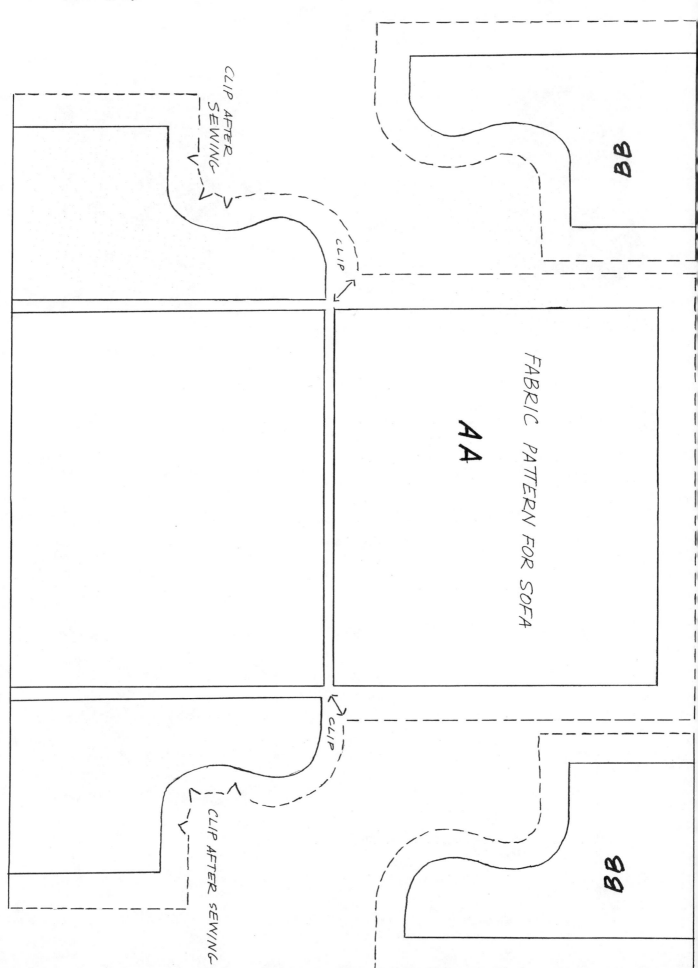

CLIP AFTER SEWING

CLIP

FABRIC PATTERN FOR SOFA

AA

BB

CLIP

CLIP AFTER SEWING

BB

3. Place 1/4" thick padding on the top section, which is the front of the chair back.
4. Place pattern part C on the padding.
5. Glue the fabric edges on pattern part C.
6. Fold part C to meet the bottom edge of AA.
7. Insert A parts into fabric parts AA and glue the front edges around the balsa.

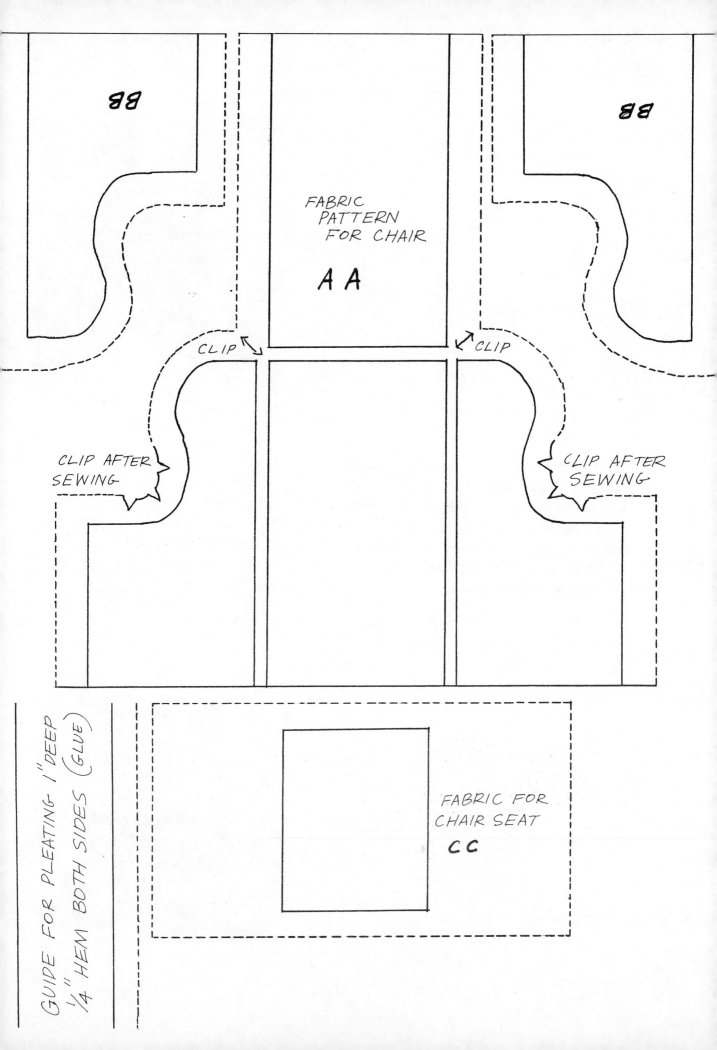

FABRIC
PATTERN
FOR CHAIR

A A

BB

BB

CLIP

CLIP

CLIP AFTER
SEWING

CLIP AFTER
SEWING

FABRIC FOR
CHAIR SEAT

C C

GUIDE FOR PLEATING- 1" DEEP
¼" HEM BOTH SIDES (GLUE)

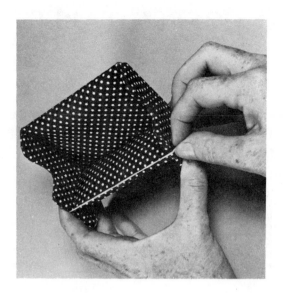

8. Pad and cover pattern part B with fabric part CC.
9. Fold the sides of the chair to form a 45° angle with the back. Glue in the seat section and hold with a tight rubber band until dry.
10. Glue the top and bottom hems on DD. Fold into pleats.
11. Glue each pleat of the DD sections into place on the chair. Hold with a rubber band until dry.

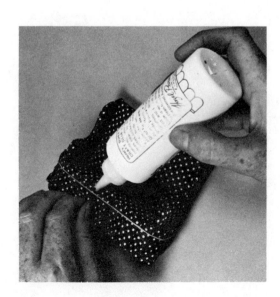

4 COFFEE TABLE

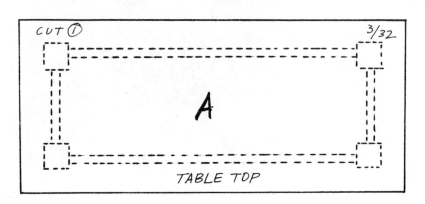

CUT ①   3/32

A

TABLE TOP

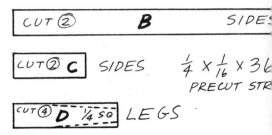

CUT ②   **B**   SIDES

CUT ② **C**   SIDES $\frac{1}{4} \times \frac{1}{16} \times 36$

PRECUT STR

CUT ④ **D** $\frac{1}{4}$ SQ   LEGS

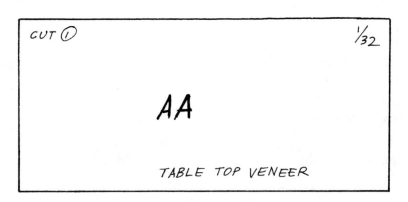

CUT ①   1/32

AA

TABLE TOP VENEER

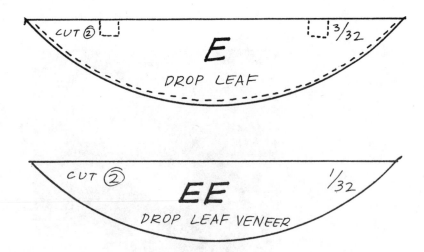

CUT ②   3/32

E

DROP LEAF

CUT ②   1/32

EE

DROP LEAF VENEER

Supplies

balsa wood
   3/32" x 3" x 36"
   1/32" x 3" x 36"
   1/16" x 1/4" x 36" (precut strip)
two glue-on hinges

Instructions

1. Cut out all pattern parts on the pattern sheet.
2. Sand pattern parts A and AA and half-round both ends, leaving the sides straight.
3. Sand pattern parts E and EE and half-round the outside edges, leaving a straight edge for the hinges to join top and leaf.

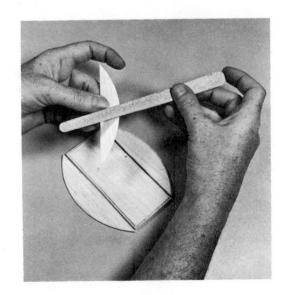

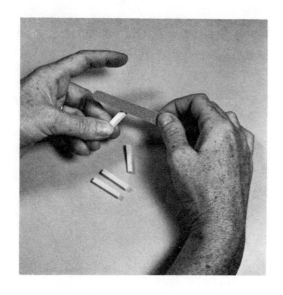

4. Sand all sides of B and C parts.
5. Shave and sand D parts, using the dotted lines on pattern part D as a guide.

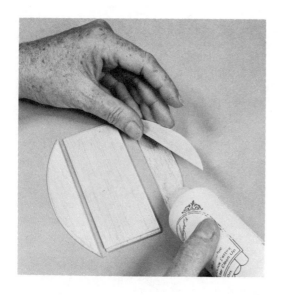

6. Stain all parts.
7. Glue part AA to the top of A. Glue parts EE to the tops of E.

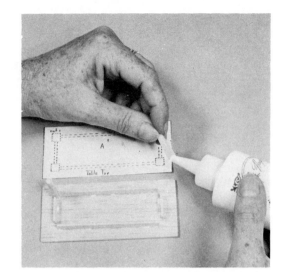

8. Using the dotted lines on pattern part A as a guide, glue parts B, C, and D into place.
9. Let dry thoroughly.

10. Glue hinges on the underside of A and join two E pattern parts as indicated on the dotted lines.
11. Let dry thoroughly.
12. Varnish with two coats.

5 ROUND TABLE

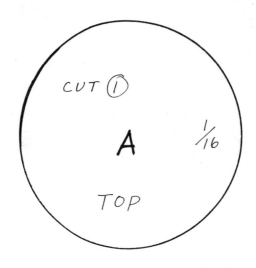

CUT ①

A

$\frac{1}{16}$

TOP

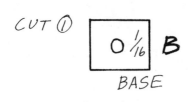

CUT ①

O $\frac{1}{16}$ B

BASE

ARROWS INDICATE SCORE MARKS

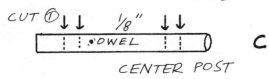

CUT ① ↓↓ $\frac{1}{8}$" ↓↓

DOWEL

C

CENTER POST

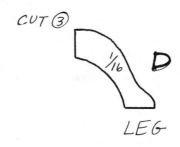

CUT ③

$\frac{1}{16}$ D

LEG

Supplies

1/16" x 3" x 36" balsa
1/8" (round) x 36" dowel

Instructions

1. Cut out all pieces on the pattern sheet. Make a
   hole in the center of pattern part B to hold the
   center post.
2. Sand all pieces, taking particular care with
   pattern parts D. Cut a few extra feet just in case.
   Place the small foot on a flat piece of a 1/2"
   balsa strip.

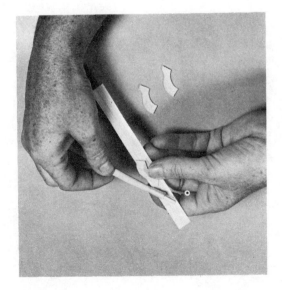

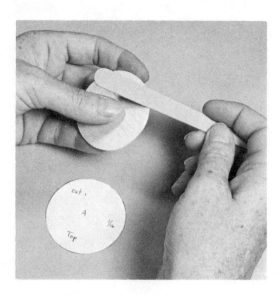

3. Half-round the top edges of the tabletop (pattern part A). Sand and full-round the tops of pattern parts D.

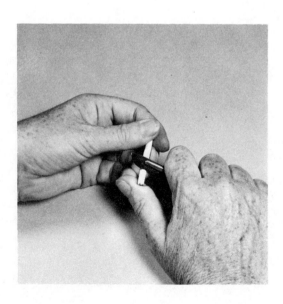

4. Score the center post (part C).

5. Stain all pattern parts.

6. Glue pattern part B, the base, to the bottom of part A, the top. Remember that the top part of the tabletop is half-rounded. Let dry thoroughly.

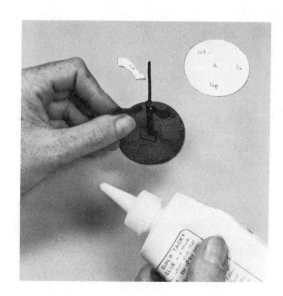

7. Glue the legs (pattern parts D) to the lower edge of the dowel (pattern part C). Put the table upside down on a flat surface. With the dowel straight up, position the legs around the dowel, forming a Y shape. Hold the legs in position until the glue starts to set before positioning the next leg.
8. Let the complete table dry thoroughly.
9. Varnish with two coats.

❻ DESK

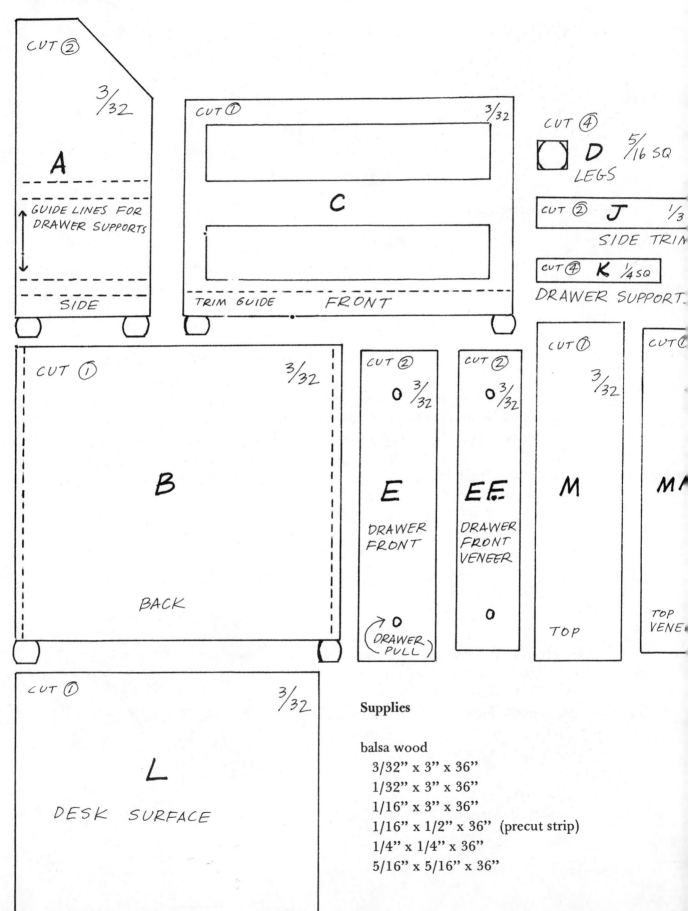

CUT ②

3/32

A

GUIDE LINES FOR
DRAWER SUPPORTS

SIDE

CUT ①   3/32

C

TRIM GUIDE   FRONT

CUT ④
☐ **D** 5/16 SQ
LEGS

CUT ② J 1/3
SIDE TRIM

CUT ④ K 1/4 SQ
DRAWER SUPPORT.

CUT ①   3/32

B

BACK

CUT ②
O 3/32

E

DRAWER
FRONT

↗ O
(DRAWER
PULL)

CUT ②
O 3/32

E E.

DRAWER
FRONT
VENEER

O

CUT ①
3/32

M

TOP

CUT ①

M

TOP
VENE

CUT ①   3/32

L

DESK SURFACE

Supplies

balsa wood
  3/32" x 3" x 36"
  1/32" x 3" x 36"
  1/16" x 3" x 36"
  1/16" x 1/2" x 36" (precut strip)
  1/4" x 1/4" x 36"
  5/16" x 5/16" x 36"

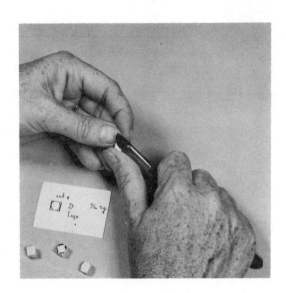

Instructions

1. Cut all pattern parts on the pattern sheet.
2. Sand all straight edges.
   Half-round parts M on the outer surface.
   Half-round parts MM (veneer) on the outer surface.
   Carve down and sand parts D.
   Miter the end edges of parts I and J (veneer).
   Half-round parts E.
   Half-round parts EE.

ONT. DESK PATTERN —

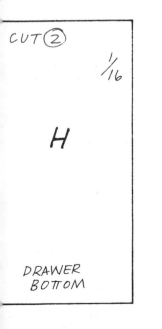

CUT ②

1/16

H

DRAWER BOTTOM

CUT ②

1/16

F

DRAWER BACK

CUT ④

G

DRAWER SIDE

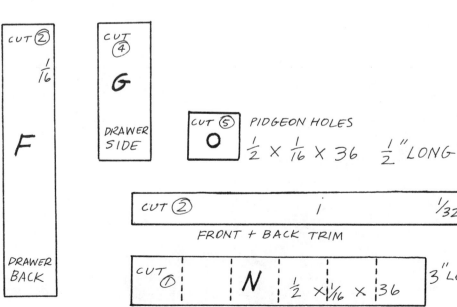

CUT ⑤   PIDGEON HOLES

O $\frac{1}{2} \times \frac{1}{16} \times 36$ $\frac{1}{2}$" LONG

CUT ②   i   1/32

FRONT + BACK TRIM

CUT ①   N $\frac{1}{2} \times \frac{1}{16} \times 36$ 3" LONG

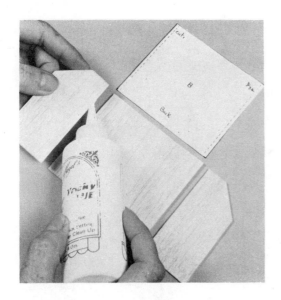

3. Stain the outside of all parts A, B, C, E, I, J, O, P, L, EE, and MM.
4. Stain both sides of all parts D, N, and O.
5. Using the dotted lines on part B as a guide, glue A and C to B.

6. Glue in part L.
7. Glue parts D (four legs) in place.
8. Glue EE to E.

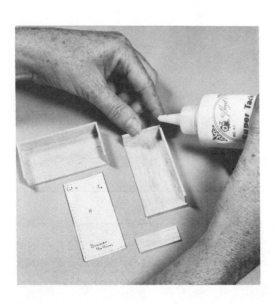

9. Glue MM to M.
10. Glue five parts O along the dotted lines of part N.
11. Glue pigeonholes to the inside of the top (hanging down).

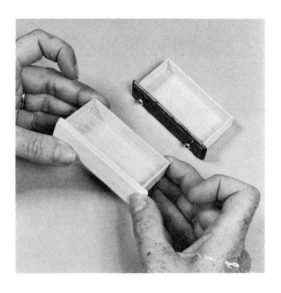

12. To assemble the drawers, use pattern part H as a guide and glue one G and two F parts to one H part. Repeat for the second drawer.

13. Center and glue on the drawer front. Add beads for pulls.

14. Using the dotted lines on pattern part A, glue the drawer guides into place. Let dry and insert drawers

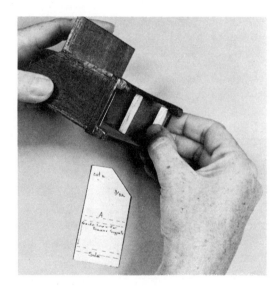

15. Glue parts I and J along the bottom, using the dotted lines on pattern parts A and B as a guide.

16. Varnish with two coats. Let dry thoroughly.

17. Use the corners of regular envelopes to represent letters in the cubbyholes.

7 LADDERBACK CHAIR

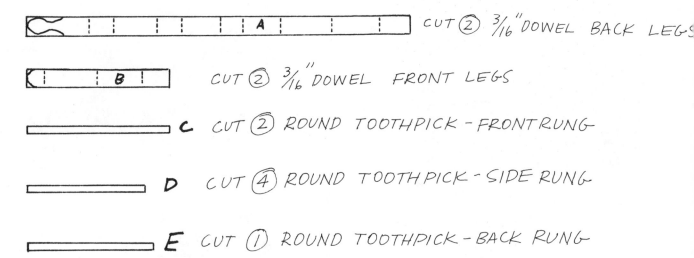

CUT ② 3/16" DOWEL BACK LEGS

CUT ② 3/16" DOWEL FRONT LEGS

C CUT ② ROUND TOOTHPICK - FRONT RUNG

D CUT ④ ROUND TOOTHPICK - SIDE RUNG

E CUT ① ROUND TOOTHPICK - BACK RUNG

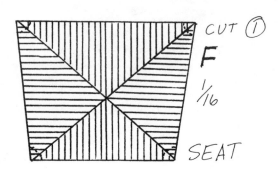

CUT ①
F
1/16

SEAT

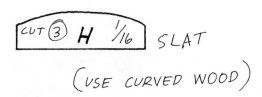

SLAT

(USE CURVED WOOD)

Supplies

bent balsa
  1/16" x 3" x 36"
  1/16" x 3" x 36"

3/16" dowel
round toothpicks

Instructions

1. Cut out all pattern parts on the pattern sheet. Cut pattern parts H from bent wood.
2. Score the legs by running a sharp knife or an X-Acto knife around the dowel as marked on the pattern. Using the flat edge of a file or emery board, make the scoring marks more pronounced. Carve the top of the leg backs as marked on the pattern.

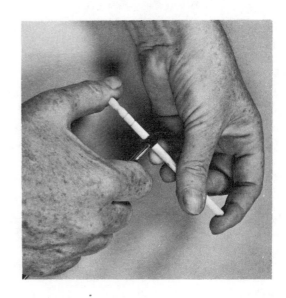

3. Mark pattern part F with the back of an X-Acto knife to look like a rush seat, using a ruler. Follow the pattern to obtain the desired look.
4. Sand all parts. Half-round the top edge of pattern part F.
5. Stain all parts.

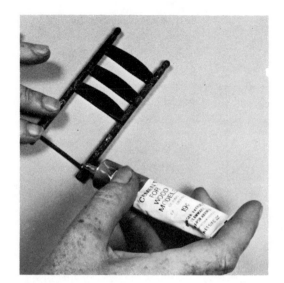

6. Place pattern parts A on a flat surface. Glue parts H and E between back legs, using the scoring mark as a guide. Let dry thoroughly.

7. Place pattern parts B on a flat surface. Glue parts C between the front legs. Let dry thoroughly.

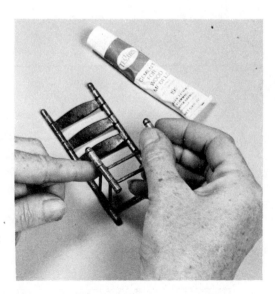

8. Join the front section to the back section by gluing pattern parts D into place.
9. Place pattern part F in position and glue. Let dry thoroughly.
10. Varnish the completed chair with two coats.

8 HARVEST TABLE

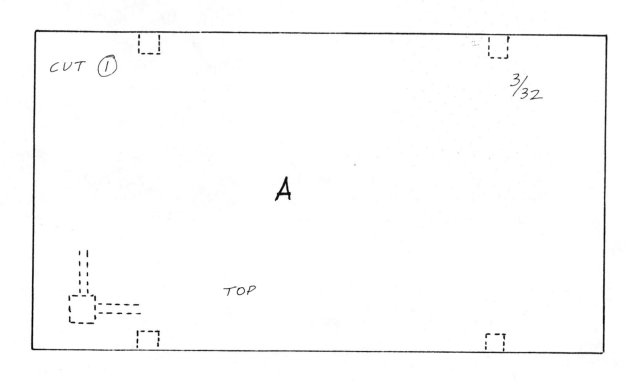

CUT ①

3/32

A

TOP

B

DROP LEAF

3/32

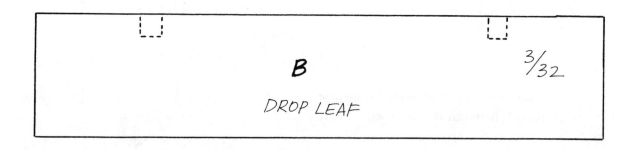

CUT ②   C   SIDE SUPPORT

CUT ②   D $\frac{3}{32} \times \frac{1}{4} \times 36$ END SUPPORT

E

CUT ④   LEG

Supplies

balsa wood
   3/32" x 1/4" x 36" (precut strip)
   1/4" x 1/4" x 36"
   3/32" x 4" x 36"
   four hinges

Instructions

1. Cut out all pattern pieces on the pattern sheet.
2. Sand all pattern parts. Half-round the end edges of part A, leaving the side that joins the leaves with the hinges straight.

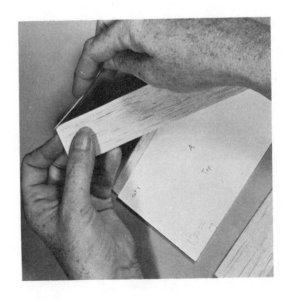

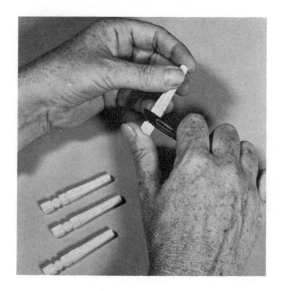

3. Sand and half-round one long and two short side edges of pattern parts B. Leave the sides that join the table with hinges straight.
4. Carve four E pattern parts as follows: score as marked with an X-Acto knife, shave down the rounded portion, and sand down the bottom part of the leg to obtain a tapered look.

5. Stain all pattern parts.
6. On the underside of pattern piece A glue parts C and D as marked on the pattern.

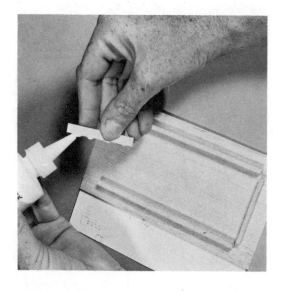

7. Hinge pattern part B to pattern part A as marked on the pattern.

8. Glue pattern part H (legs) into position.
9. Let dry thoroughly.
10. Varnish with two coats, sanding lightly after each.

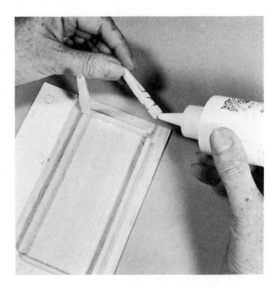

⑨ CORNER CABINET

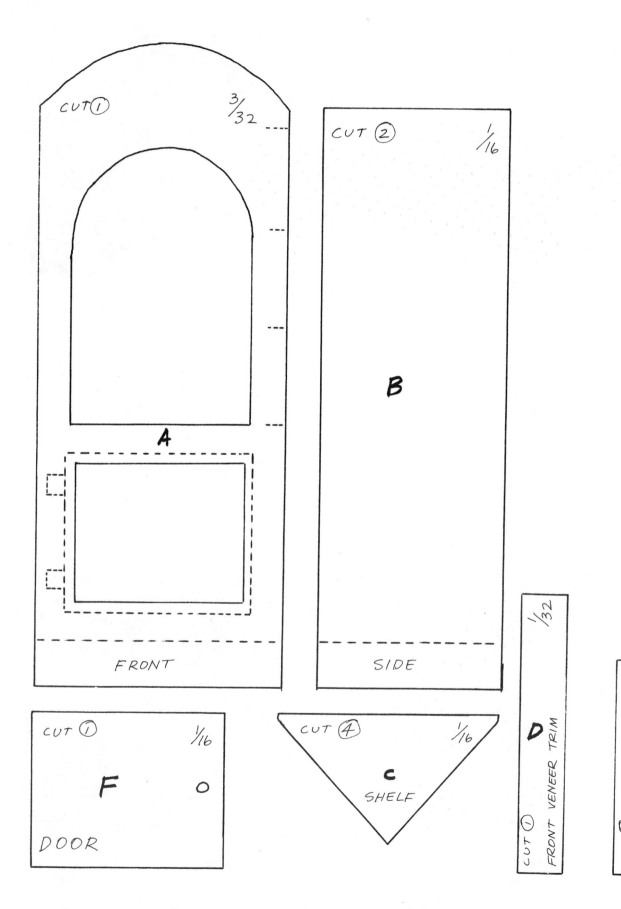

CUT ①   3/32

A

FRONT

CUT ①   1/16

F   O

DOOR

CUT ②   1/16

B

SIDE

CUT ④   1/16

C

SHELF

1/32

D

CUT ①   FRONT VENEER TRIM

1/32

E

CUT ②   SIDE VENEER TRIM

Supplies

balsa wood
   3/32" x 3" x 36"
   1/32" x 3" x 36"
   1/16" x 3" x 36"
two glue-on hinges
one gold bead

Instructions

1. Cut out all pattern parts on the pattern sheet.
2. Sand all parts. Half-round parts F and the top of parts A, D, and two Es.

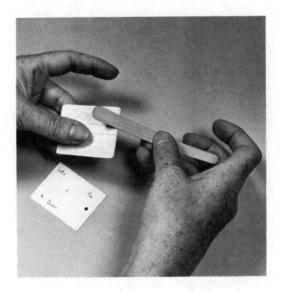

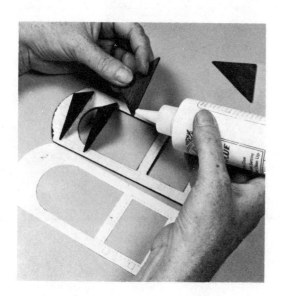

3. Miter the sides of parts A, B, D, and two Es.
4. Stain or paint all parts.
5. Using the dotted lines on pattern part A as a guide, glue parts C.

6. Glue the backs of part B to part A.

7. Glue parts D and two Es into place, using the dotted lines as a guide.
8. Using small glue-on hinges, glue the doors into place. Put the hinges outside the corner cabinet and inside the doors. Add one bead for the door pull.
9. Varnish with two coats.

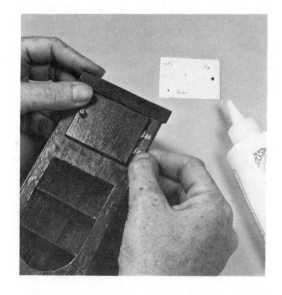

10 DEACON'S BENCH

Supplies

3/32" x 3" x 36" balsa

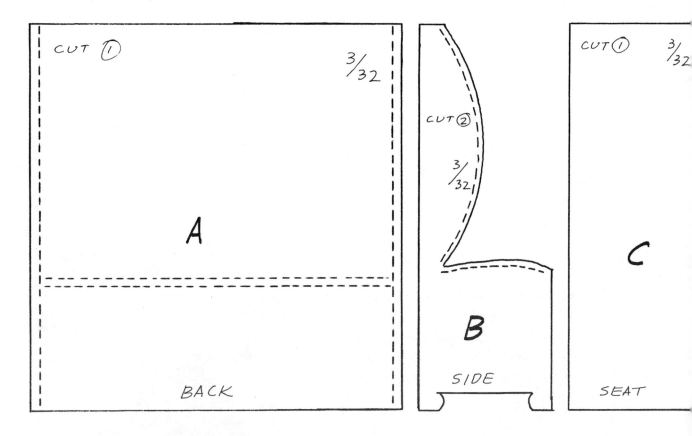

CUT ①   3/32

A

BACK

CUT ②   3/32

B

SIDE

CUT ①   3/32

C

SEAT

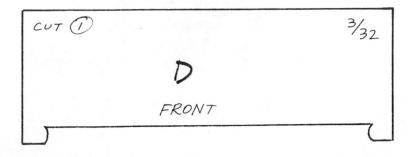

CUT ①   3/32

D

FRONT

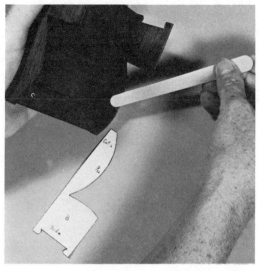

Instructions

1. Cut out all pattern parts from the pattern sheet.
2. Sand all pattern parts. Full-round the front sides of parts B as indicated on the dotted lines.

3. Stain all parts.
4. Using pattern part A as a guide, glue parts B to A.

5. Glue part C to A.
6. Glue part D to front parts B and C.
7. Let dry thoroughly.
8. Varnish with two coats.
9. Slightly pad the cushion to fit pattern part C.

11 CANOPY BED

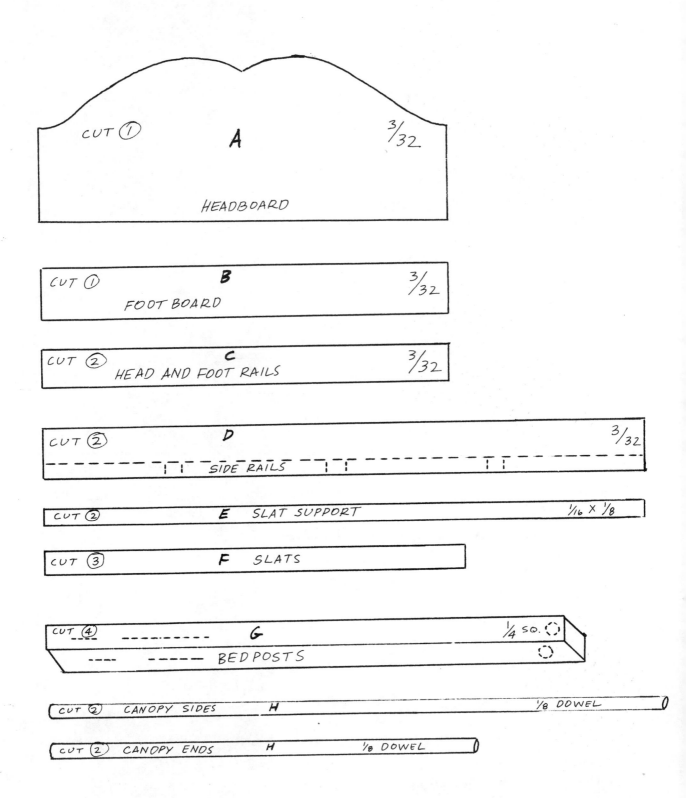

CUT ①   **A**   3/32

HEADBOARD

CUT ①   **B**   3/32

FOOT BOARD

CUT ②   **C**   3/32

HEAD AND FOOT RAILS

CUT ②   **D**   3/32

SIDE RAILS

CUT ②   **E**   SLAT SUPPORT   1/16 X 1/8

CUT ③   **F**   SLATS

CUT ④   **G**   1/4 SQ.

BEDPOSTS

CUT ②   CANOPY SIDES   **H**   1/8 DOWEL

CUT ②   CANOPY ENDS   **H**   1/8 DOWEL

Supplies

balsa wood
   3/32" x 4" x 36" (strip)
   1/16" x 1/2" (precut strip)
   1/16" x 1/4" (precut strip)
   1/16" x 1/8" (precut strip)
   5/16" square

1/2" foam
1/8" x 36" dowel

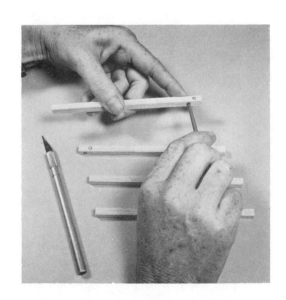

Instructions

1. Cut out all pattern parts from the pattern sheet.
2. Sand all parts. Round the top edge of A.
3. Make holes in the tops of the bed posts (part G)
   to hold the canopy dowels (marked on pattern).

ALLOW ¼ INCH MORE FOR HEM. CUT ON DOTTED
LINE INTO CORNER TO ALLOW TURNING.

← STITCH LINE

¼"

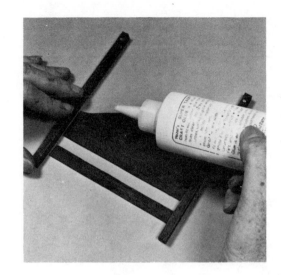

4. Stain parts A, B, C, D, G, and H.
5. Join two G parts by gluing A (headboard) and one C part together. Join two more G parts by gluing B and another C part together.
6. Glue E parts to the bottom edge of Ds as indicated on the dotted line. Let dry thoroughly.
7. Glue Ds to the front and back sections of the bed. Let dry thoroughly.

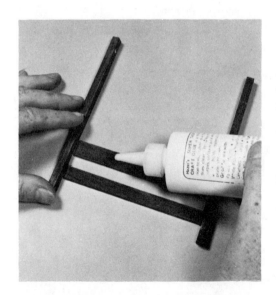

8. Place and glue pattern parts F (bed slats) to pattern parts E as indicated on the dotted line.

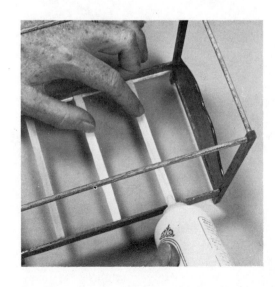

ALLOW ¼ INCH MORE FOR HEM. CUT ON DOTTED
LINE INTO CORNER TO ALLOW TURNING

¼ "

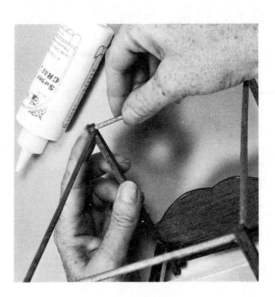

9. Connect four G parts with H parts (dowel) to form canopy.

10. Varnish the stained parts of the bed with two coats.

11. To make the mattress and pillow, cut out a piece of 1/2" x 4" x 6" foam for the mattress, and 1/2" x 1¼" x 4" for the pillow.

12 DRESSER

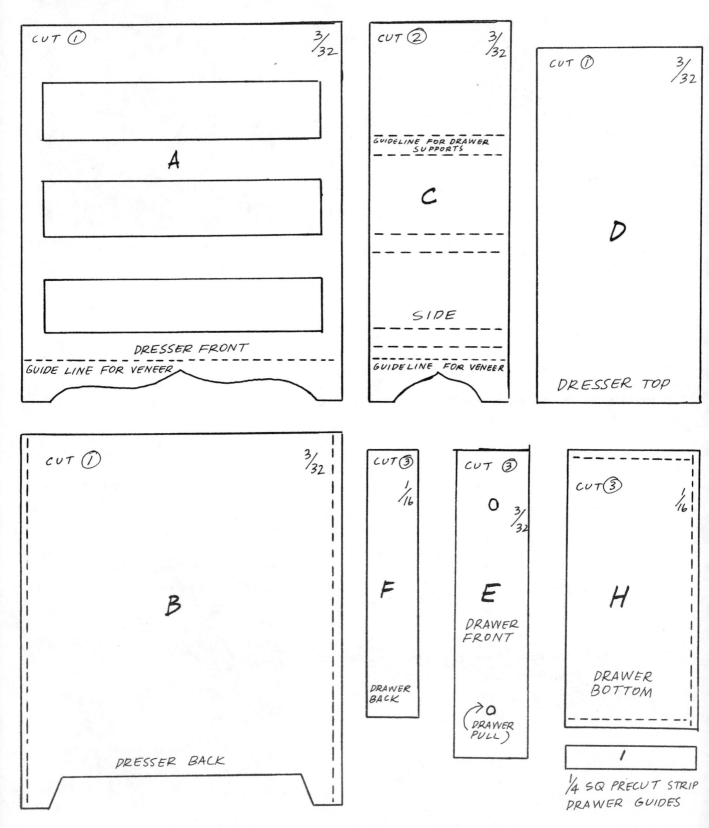

CUT ①   3/32

A

DRESSER FRONT

GUIDE LINE FOR VENEER

CUT ②   3/32

GUIDELINE FOR DRAWER SUPPORTS

C

SIDE

GUIDELINE FOR VENEER

CUT ①   3/32

D

DRESSER TOP

CUT ①   3/32

B

DRESSER BACK

CUT ③   1/16

F

DRAWER BACK

CUT ③

O

E   3/32

DRAWER FRONT

O (DRAWER PULL)

CUT ③   1/16

H

DRAWER BOTTOM

I

1/4 SQ PRECUT STRIP DRAWER GUIDES

Supplies

balsa wood

    1/32" x 3" x 36"
    3/32" x 4" x 36"
    1/16" x 3" x 36"
    1/16" x 1/8" x 36" (precut strip)

six beads for drawer pulls

Instructions

1. Cut out all pattern pieces from the pattern sheet.
2. Sand all pieces. Half-round pattern parts D, E, DD, and EE.
3. Stain the outside of parts A, B, C, D, E, DD, and EE.
4. Using pattern part B as a guide, glue pattern parts C to B along the dotted lines. Glue pattern part A to parts C.

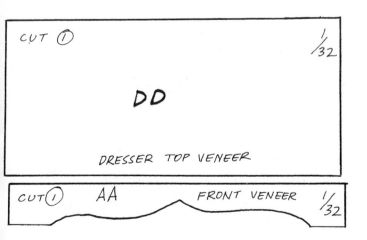

CUT ①   1/32

DD

DRESSER TOP VENEER

CUT ①   AA   FRONT VENEER   1/32

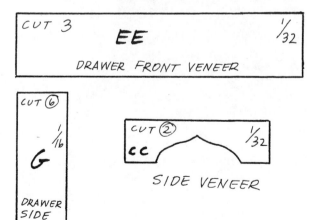

CUT 3   **EE**   1/32

DRAWER FRONT VENEER

CUT ⑥   1/16   **G**   DRAWER SIDE

CUT ②   1/32   **cc**

SIDE VENEER

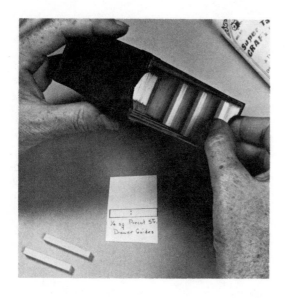

5. Glue parts I to the inside of C along the dotted lines. Glue parts DD to D and EE to E.

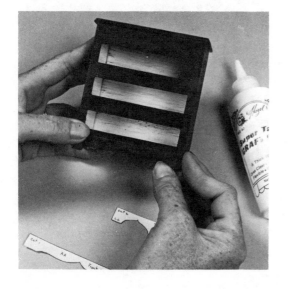

6. Glue part D to the top of assembled parts A, B, and C.
7. Glue parts AA and CC to the front and sides of the dresser along the dotted lines.

8. Let dry thoroughly.
9. Assemble the drawers as follows: using pattern part H as a pattern, join parts F and G to form the drawer; center the drawer and glue on the drawer front; glue on beads for drawer knobs as indicated on pattern piece E.
10. Let the drawers dry thoroughly.
11. Varnish the completed dresser with two coats.

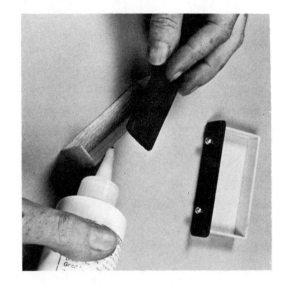

13 CRADLE

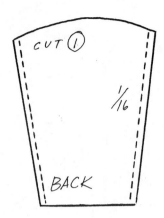

CUT ① 1/16

BACK

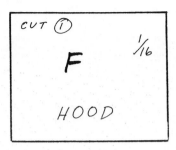

CUT ① F 1/16

HOOD

USE "BENT" BALSA WOOD FOR PART
F. DIRECTIONS FOR BENDING BALSA
WOOD ARE IN THE FRONT SECTION
OF THIS BOOK.

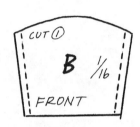

CUT① B 1/16

FRONT

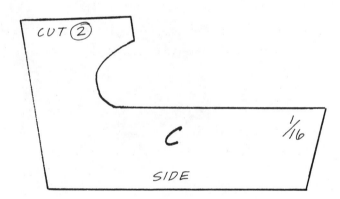

CUT ② C 1/16

SIDE

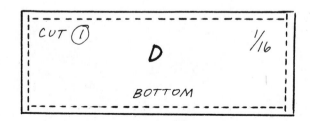

CUT ① D 1/16

BOTTOM

CUT ② E 1/16

ROCKER

Supplies

1/16" x 3" x 36" balsa

Instructions

1. Cut out all pieces on the pattern sheet.
2. Sand the outside edges of C along the bottom to fit D. The sides of the cradle slant out slightly and are fitted to a flat surface. Sand and slightly round the *top* edges of A, B, and two Cs. Sand and slightly round the *bottom* edges of two Es. Stain all pieces before glueing.

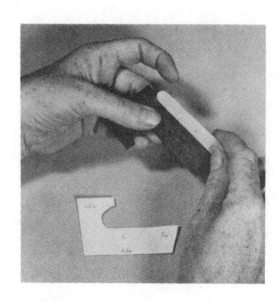

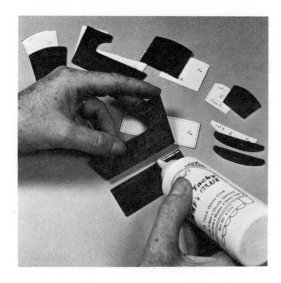

3. Place the bottom (part D) on a flat surface and use the dotted lines as a guide for glueing.

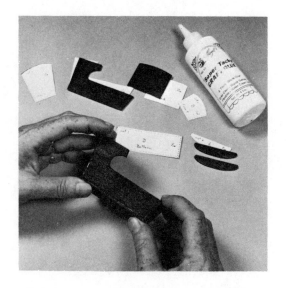

4. Glue pattern parts A and B to the opposite ends of D.
5. Glue pattern parts C to the opposite sides of D. Glue A and B at the same time.

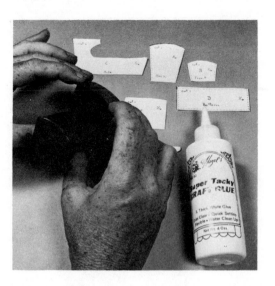

6. Glue the top of part F to the top of pattern parts C. Use bent wood for F.

7. Glue parts E to the bottom of the cradle 1/2" from each end.
8. Let dry thoroughly.
9. Varnish with two coats.

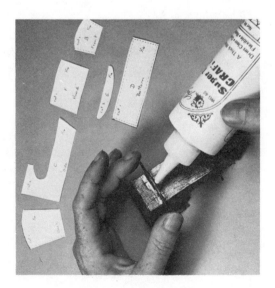

14 BLANKET CHEST

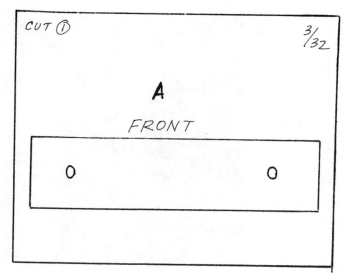

CUT ①   3/32

A

FRONT

0   0

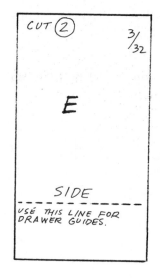

CUT ②   3/32

E

SIDE

USE THIS LINE FOR
DRAWER GUIDES.

CUT ①   1/16

0

F

0

DRAWER
FRONT

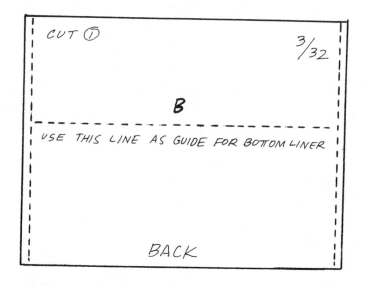

CUT ①   3/32

B

USE THIS LINE AS GUIDE FOR BOTTOM LINER

BACK

CUT ①   1/16

H

DRAWER BOTTOM

CUT ①   1/16

I

DRAWER
BACK

CUT ②

K

1/16

FRONT AND BACK VENEER

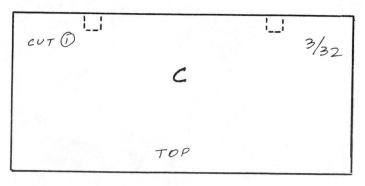

CUT ①   3/32

C

TOP

CUT ②   L   1/16
SIDE VENEER

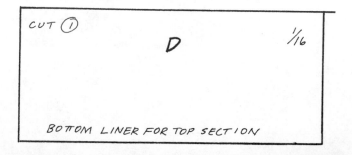

CUT ①   1/16

D

BOTTOM LINER FOR TOP SECTION

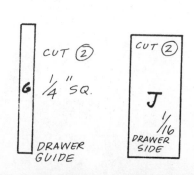

CUT ②

G   1/4" SQ.

DRAWER
GUIDE

CUT ②

J

1/16
DRAWER
SIDE

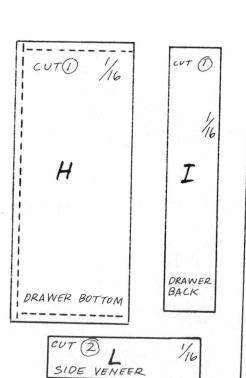

Supplies

balsa wood
 3/32" x 3" x 36"
 1/16" x 3" x 36"
 1/4" x 1/4" x 36"

two small glue-on hinges
two small wooden beads

Instructions

1. Cut out all pattern parts on the sheet.
2. Sand all straight edges with an emery board. Half-round pattern parts C and the top edge of K and L.
3. Paint all outside pieces (A, B, C, E, and F). The sides, back, and bottom drawer (J, I, and H) are not painted, nor is the bottom liner of the top section (D).
4. Using the dotted lines on pattern piece B (back) as a guide, start glueing. Glue both sides (E) and the bottom liner for the top section (D) to the back (B).

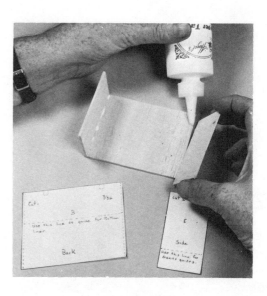

DECORATIONS: PENNSYLVANIA DUTCH MOTIF FOR BLANKET CHEST

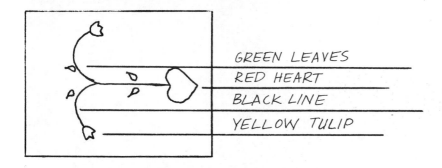

GREEN LEAVES
RED HEART
BLACK LINE
YELLOW TULIP

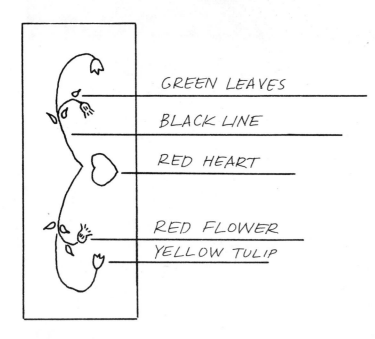

GREEN LEAVES

BLACK LINE

RED HEART

RED FLOWER
YELLOW TULIP

USE OLD FASHION RUBBING METHOD TO TRANSFER PATTERN TO PAINTED BLANKET CHEST. RUB BACK OF PICTURE WITH SOFT PENCIL. RUBBED SIDE DOWN, TRACE PATTERN OVER WITH HARD LEAD PENCIL, THEN PAINT.

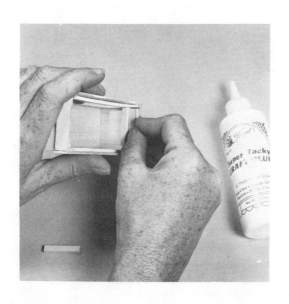

5. Glue pattern parts G to the insides of parts E as marked.
6. Glue A to the front of sides E.
7. Glue on the lower veneer as marked on the pattern.
8. To assemble the drawer, use the drawer bottom (pattern part H) as a guide, and glue drawer parts I (back) and two Js (drawer sides) in place. Glue the front of the drawer (pattern piece F) to the body.

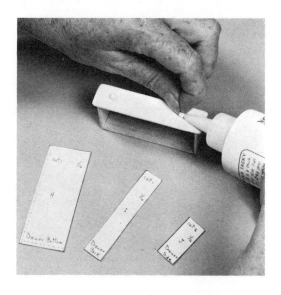

9. Glue on drawer pulls (beads) in the appropriate spots (marked on pattern piece F).

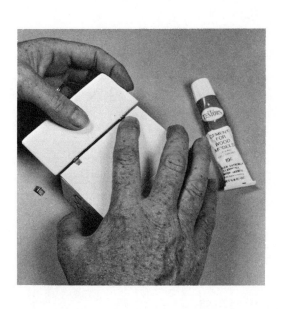

10. Glue on hinges in the appropriate spots (marked on pattern piece C). They go on the outside of pattern piece B and underneath pattern piece C.

11. Varnish with two coats.

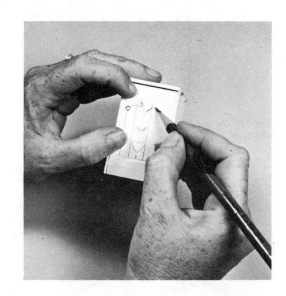

12. An alternate finish for the blanket chest is to omit steps (3) and (10) and to paint the chest white, antique gold, blue, or green; let dry thoroughly; using the Pennsylvania Dutch stencil, paint the front and sides with acrylic paint; let dry thoroughly; and varnish with two coats..

15 FOLDING SCREEN

Supplies

balsa wood
   1/16" x 3" x 36"
   1/16" x 3/16" x 36" (precut strip)

miniature wallpaper
four glue-on craft hinges

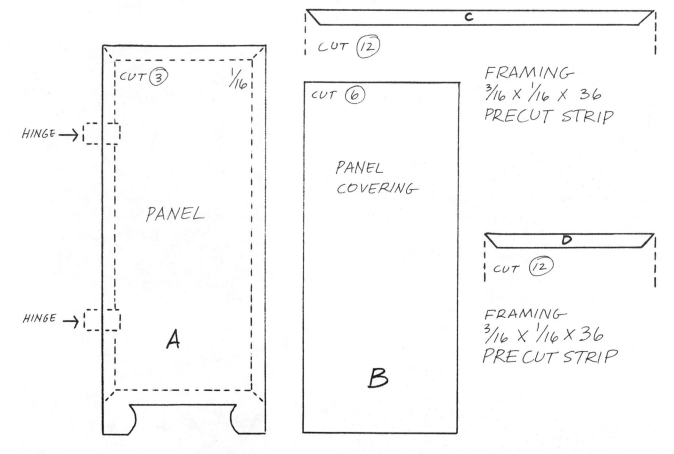

C

CUT ⑫

FRAMING
3/16 X 1/16 X 36
PRECUT STRIP

CUT ③   1/16

HINGE →

PANEL

CUT ⑥

PANEL
COVERING

HINGE →

A

B

D

CUT ⑫

FRAMING
3/16 X 1/16 X 36
PRE CUT STRIP

APPLY HINGES ON PANEL ONE AND PANEL TWO AS MARKED ON
PATTERN SHEET.
APPLY SECOND SET OF HINGES ON OPPOSITE SIDE OF FIRST SET.
TAKE FIRST TWO HINGED PANELS AND PLACE HINGE DOWN ON FLAT
SURFACE AND THEN ADD LAST PANEL.

Instructions

1. Cut out all pattern parts on the pattern sheet.
2. Sand all wood parts. Miter the ends of all C and D parts.
3. Stain all C and D parts and the feet and edges of three A parts.
4. Glue wallpaper on both sides of three A parts using thick, white craft glue diluted with water to the consistency of wallpaper paste.

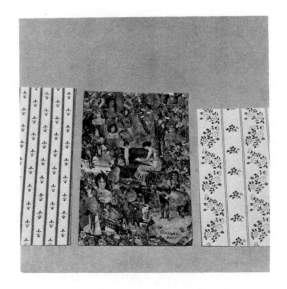

5. Let dry thoroughly.
6. Glue on hinges as indicated on the pattern.
7. Varnish the wood parts and let dry. Sand lightly and revarnish.

16 TWIN BED

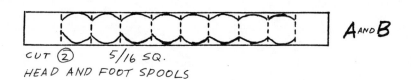

A AND B

CUT ②   5/16 SQ.
HEAD AND FOOT SPOOLS

CUT ②
     HEAD AND FOOT RAILS   3/32 C

CUT ②   SIDE RAILS   1/2 × 1/16 × 36 D
PRE CUT STRIP

CUT ②   SLAT SUPPORT   1/8 × 1/16 × 36 E
PRECUT STRIP

CUT ③   SLAT   1/4 × 1/16 × 36 F
PRECUT STRIP

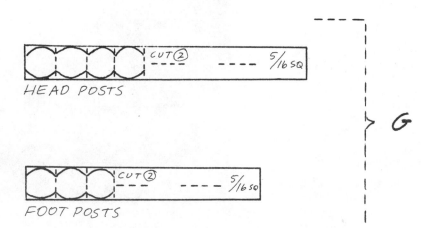

HEAD POSTS   CUT ②   5/16 SQ

G

FOOT POSTS   CUT ②   5/16 SQ

Supplies

balsa wood

  3/32" x 4" x 36"
  1/16" x 1/2" x 36" (precut strip)
  1/16" x 1/4" x 36" (precut strip)
  1/16" x 1/8" x 36" (precut strip)
  5/16" square

1/2" thick foam

Instructions

1. Cut out all pattern parts from the pattern sheet.
2. Sand all parts. Carve and sand parts A, B, and G.

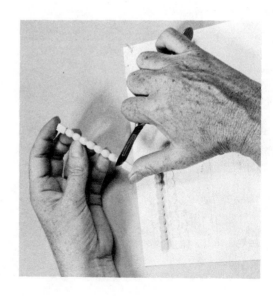

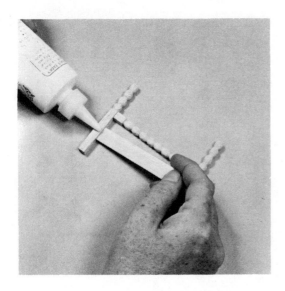

3. Stain parts A, B, C, D, and G.
4. Join two G parts to one A and one C part to form the headboard. Join two more G parts with one B and one C part to form the footboard. Let dry thoroughly.

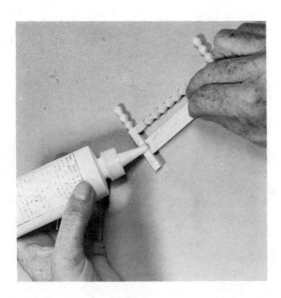

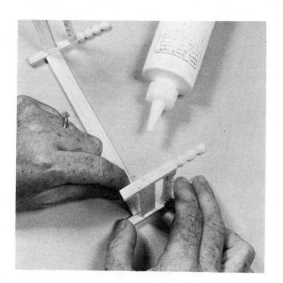

5. Glue E parts to the bottom edge of D parts along the dotted line. Let dry thoroughly.
6. Glue D parts to the front and back sections of the bed as indicated on pattern part G. Let dry thoroughly.

7. Glue pattern parts F (bed slats) to pattern parts E.
8. Apply two coats of finish to the bed.
9. To make the mattress and pillow, cut out a piece of 1/2" x 3½" x 6" foam for the mattress, 1/2" x 1¼" x 3½" for the pillow.

17 FOOTSTOOL

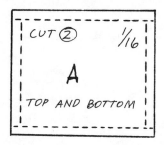

CUT ② 1/16
A
TOP AND BOTTOM

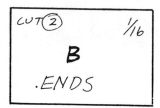

CUT ② 1/16
B
.ENDS

CUT ② 1/16
C
FRONT AND BACK

FABRIC TO
COVER TOP

1/4 INCH HEM

GUIDE FOR PLEATS

1/4 INCH HEM

Supplies

1/16" x 3" x 36" balsa
fabric
padding

Instructions

1. Cut out all pattern parts on the pattern sheet.
2. Using pattern part A as a guide, glue two ends (pattern parts B) into place.
3. Glue the front and back (pattern parts C) into place.

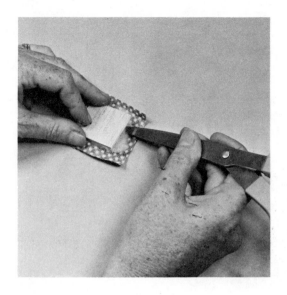

4. Apply a small amount of padding to the remaining A part (top of footstool). Glue the padding into place and put it face down on the wrong side of the fabric (pattern part D). Glue securely.

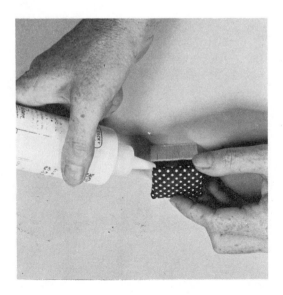

5. Glue the completed top to assembled parts A, B, and C.

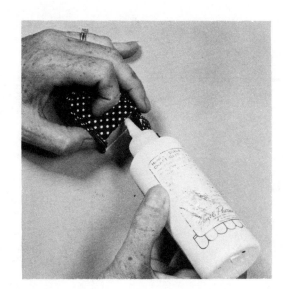

6. Make a pleated or ruffled skirt the same height as the stool and glue into place. Follow the instructions for the sofa and chair (chapter 3).

18 CORNER SHELF

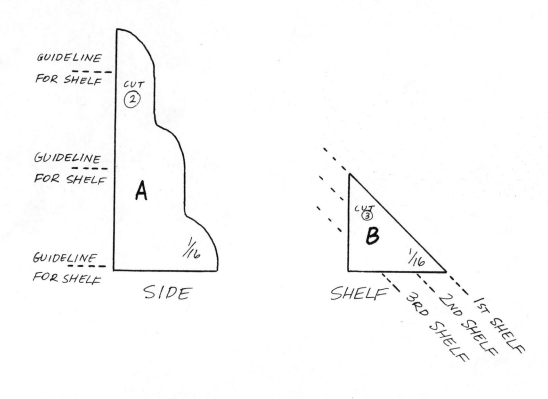

ALTERNATE SHELF PATTERNS TO BE USED WITH A's TO MAKE BOOKSHELF.

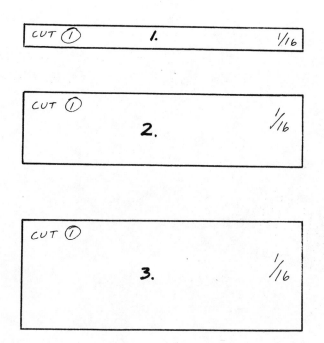

Supplies

1/16" x 3" x 36" balsa

Instructions

1. Cut out all pieces from the pattern sheet.
2. Sand and half-round two A parts.
   Sand the straight edges of three B parts.
   Miter each edge of two A parts to fit plumb.
3. Stain all parts.
4. Using the pattern as a guide, glue in shelves.
5. Let dry thoroughly.
6. Varnish and let dry.
7. Sand with fine sandpaper and revarnish.

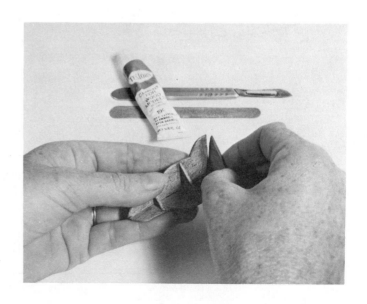

19 ROCKING HORSE

Supplies

3/32" x 3" x 36" balsa
1/8" dowel
paper or fabric

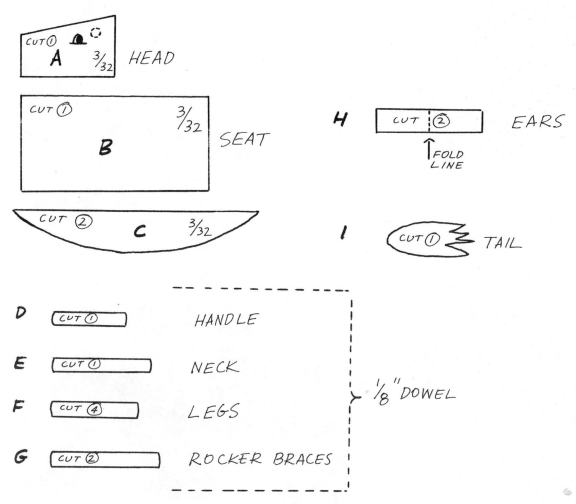

CUT①   A   3/32   HEAD

CUT①   B   3/32   SEAT

H   CUT ②   EARS   ↑ FOLD LINE

CUT ②   C   3/32

I   CUT①   TAIL

D   CUT①   HANDLE

E   CUT①   NECK

F   CUT④   LEGS

G   CUT②   ROCKER BRACES

1/8" DOWEL

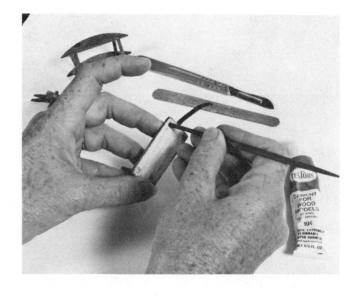

Instructions

1. Cut out all pieces from the pattern
   sheet.
2. Sand all parts.
   Round the corners of A, B, and C.

3. Make holes in the parts as indicated.
   The hole in pattern part A goes straight
   through, but the others are just deep
   enough to hold the dowel securely.
4. Paint the eyes on pattern part A as
   shown.
5. Using pattern part B as a guide, glue
   parts F (legs) into place at the angle
   shown.
6. Put the rocker braces (G parts) into
   place and join to part B.

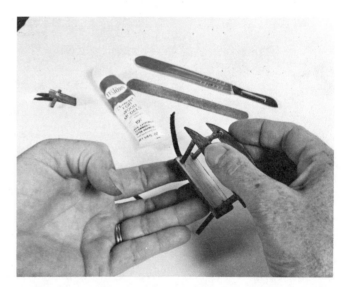

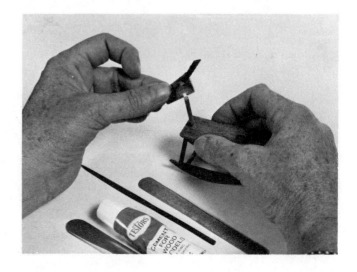

7. Set the seat and rockers upright and
   add parts E and part A.
8. Glue part D into the head.
9. Varnish and let dry thoroughly. Sand
   lightly.
10. Glue on the ears and tail.

Part III

20 ACCESSORIES AND DECORATIONS

You can make your own dollhouse or miniature-room accessories and decorations to complete your collection. They add the final authenticity you are looking for and give your dollhouse or miniature room that very important personal touch. If your home is a mirror of the people who live in it, so too is your dollhouse. Let me repeat how important it is to sign and date each piece of furniture that you make. You add to its value and help identify it in the years to come. Even your own grandchildren will appreciate knowing exactly when each piece was made. Each aspect of decorating adds a new dimension to your work. Color, for instance, can change the whole mood of a room. Let your own personality seep through in all areas. If you are trying to duplicate an authentic room, spend some time in the library looking up homes of the period. Scout out museums in your area for further information. Many pleasant hours can be spent in your research. If you are fortunate enough to have a collection of miniatures in your area, you can get many ideas and tips from well-crafted and beautiful displays.

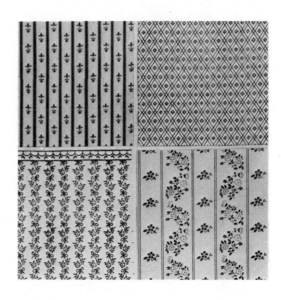

WALLPAPER

Miniature wallpapers are available in many colors and patterns. They can be purchased in craft stores where miniatures are sold. You can also buy authentic reproductions of their bigger counterparts in perfect 1"-to-1' scale.

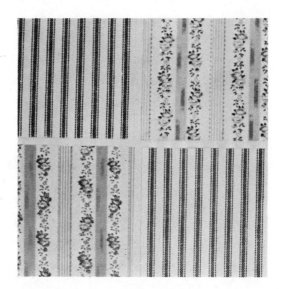

You can often use gift wrapping such as small stripes and prints. Mattress-ticking print and floral stripes come in different colors to suit your taste and color scheme.

Book-leaf liners, often referred to as Italian papers, are different and unusual. You can also use the designs as stencil patterns for both walls and floors.

SHINGLES

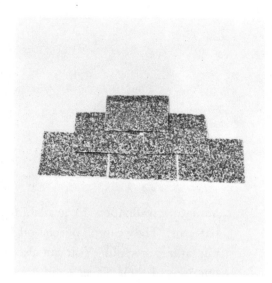

Miniature shingles can be purchased in craft stores where miniatures are sold. They are scaled to size and graduated in thickness for easy application, and the results are very professional.

You can also make shingles from coarse sandpaper cut to scale and painted the desired color. These shingles look like asphalt roofing. They are applied in the same manner as the cedar shakes.

Start at the lower edge of the roof and work upward. Vary the width of each shingle for authenticity.

CLAPBOARDS

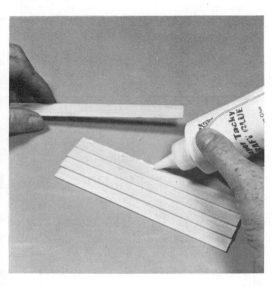

Clapboards can be made of 1/16" x 1/2" x 36" or 1/16" x 1/4" x 36" balsa strips. Cut to the desired widths and apply in the same manner as for shingles. Starting from the bottom of the surface to be covered, apply one strip at a time, overlapping slightly.

Paint them in an antique color of acrylic paint. It comes in mustard, brown, barn red, and green shades. Choose a slightly darker shade of the same color for the wood window and door trim.

COLONIAL WINDOWPANES

Pane dividers can be made from balsa strips and glued on window glass. Stain or paint the same color as the house trim.

CEILING AND FLOOR MOLDING

Molding can be purchased ready-made for dollhouses in 36" lengths, or you can make them yourself with balsa strips. Use precut 1/4" x 1/16" x 36" strips for the ceilings, and 1/2" x 1/16" x 36" for the floors. You can stain or paint them to fit the color scheme of your room.

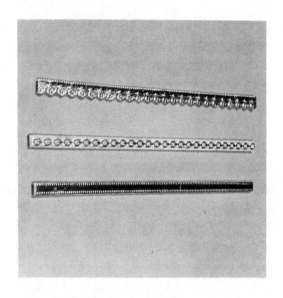

For an added touch of authenticity mark the moldings with the back of an X-Acto knife, using a ruler as a guide. Glue to the walls of your miniature room or dollhouse after you have painted or papered the walls.

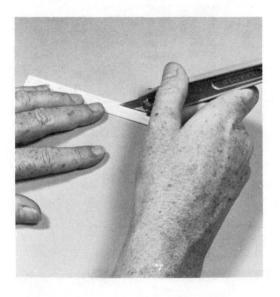

Another way to make more formal ceiling moldings is to use the fancy gold papers sold in craft stores. Glue strips over 1/4" molding and paint the same color as the woodwork. They come in scalloped and embossed motifs.

FLOORS

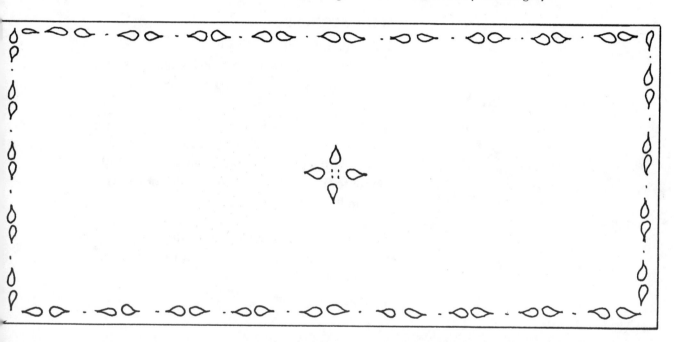

Random-width hardwood floors can be made with a ruler and a pencil. Draw the boards on a well-sanded surface and make the peg marks with a lead pencil. Penetrate the wood and twirl the pencil to get the desired size. Use a light-colored stain so that the markings show through. Varnish and let dry thoroughly.

If you wish to stencil a pattern on the floor, do so before you apply the varnish. A stencil pattern is usually applied as a border around the edge with a design in the middle.

Stencil Patterns for Painted Furniture, Walls and Floors

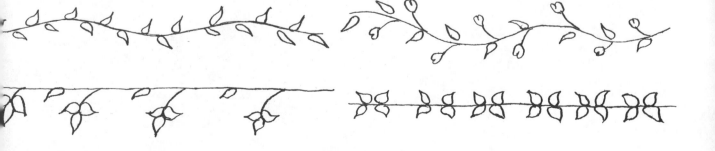

WINDOW AND CURTAIN TREATMENTS

Curtains and drapes are a very important addition to your dollhouse decorating. Calico, unbleached muslin, old laces, eyelet, satin, or old velvet found in your attic and ecru or white laces found in your fabric store are just a few materials to choose from. To make new laces look old, try dipping them in tea. Prewash any washable materials you intend to use to soften and preshrink the fabric. To make your own curtain rods, cut a piece of 1/8" dowel or a lollipop stick to the proper length and attach to the wall with small cup hooks or wire picture fasteners. The standard-size dollhouse window is 3" x 4". It can vary slightly, so be sure to measure first.

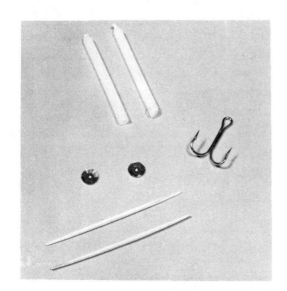

WALL SCONCES

I use single and double fish hooks for wall sconces. Glue a sequin on each point. Paint the hooks and sequins gold, pewter, or black to look like wrought iron.

To make candles, cut down and paint round toothpicks. With a pin put a hole in the bottom of the candle to fit over the point of the fish hook. Glue the candle to the fish hook.

You can also use plain white birthday candles cut to the proper size. Handmade miniature candles are also available.

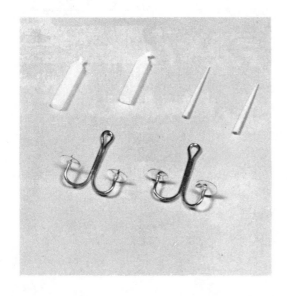

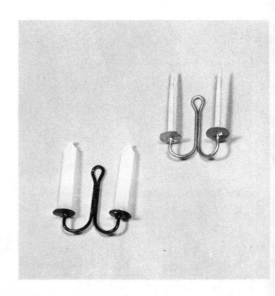

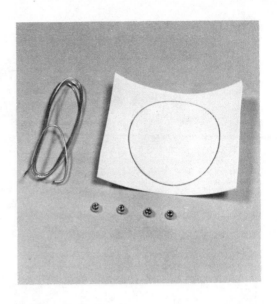

LOG CARRIERS

Cut a circle from a round plastic bottle and punch two holes on opposite sides. Bleach bottles are good for the plastic circle. The circle is approximately 2" in diameter. Using soft, bendable wire, form a handle by inserting the ends in the holes.

Bend the wire and plastic, forming opposite arcs. Glue four round beads to the bottom for feet.

Paint gold to look like brass or black to look like wrought iron. Cut up small branches to make logs.

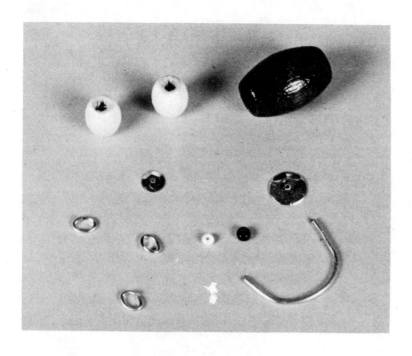

TEA SETS

Use different-size beads for the bases --
for example, 18mm for the teapot and
12mm for the sugar bowl and creamer.
All shapes and sizes can be substituted.
Use the same soft wire as for the handle
on the log carrier for the handle on the
teapot. Cut the wire to the proper size
and bend to the proper shape.

Glue to the side of the teapot base with
Duco cement. Use modeling clay for the
spout on the teapot and the lip of the
cream pitcher. Jewelry links can be used
for the handles on the creamer and sugar
bowl, and sequins with tiny beads for
the lids.

Paint and decorate with delicate flower
and fruit designs. A final coat of decoupage
finish will give them a china-like glaze.

FLOWER BOWL

Use a bead separator for the bowl. Fill with a small bit of clay. Before the clay dries, stick in tiny dried flowers to form a miniature bouquet. Craft stores have a variety of dried flowers in assorted colors. Macrame beads with large holes in the centers also make good flower containers. They can be hand-painted and finished in the same way as for the tea set.

HANGING BASKETS

Cut three equal pieces of gold chain, available in craft stores by the running foot. Join the other ends to a bead separator with more gold links. Fill the bead with modeling clay and tiny velvet leaves. You can buy the velvet leaves in bunches; separate, and cut them to the desired size.

CANDLESTICKS

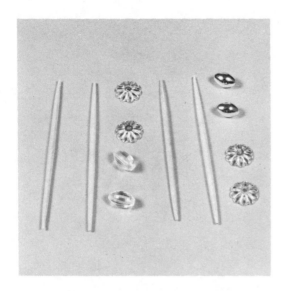
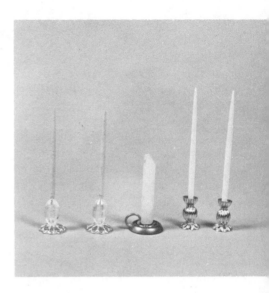

Cut down round toothpicks and paint the desired color for candles. A gold or crystal oat-shaped bead glued to a small, flat bead separator makes a beautiful candleholder. Glue the candle into the top of the oat-shaped bead. Look through jewelry-making supplies at your local craft store for many more ideas. If you make a tall candle-holding base, add a sequin to the bottom of the candle and glue on bugle beads to represent prisms.

QUILTS

There are many ways to make quilts and coverlets for doll and miniature beds. Small patchwork fabrics are available, or you can piece together your own squares. You can also applique tiny patterns. Use old pieces of lace to make an old-fashioned tester and coverlet. Lace canopies with matching spreads can turn a plain canopy bed into a beautiful treasure. With a little know-how you can make your new lace look old and treasured. Dip a brand-new quilted pattern material in tea for that antique look you have been searching for. For a filler for a miniature quilt I use a piece of flannel. Quilt batting is too thick, and not using any filler makes the quilt too flat.

RUGS

A braided rug can be made in two ways: braid yarn and sew it together like a real braided rug or crochet a single chain of wool and sew it together. Circular and oval rugs are best. Crocheted afghan rugs with fringes make a beautiful background for hand-embroidered designs. Needlepoint and petit point also make a beautiful rug. Your creativity can enhance all these ideas. Make up your own designs, and your miniatures will become your heirlooms.

SILVER CHARMS

If you are filling the corner cabinet in your miniature dining room, placing that final touch to the living-room-chair table, or just adding a personal touch to your dollhouse, use charms. There are hundreds to choose from. Personalizing a dollhouse or miniature room makes it that much more cherished.

MINIATURE BASKETS

A miniature basket filled with tiny balls of yarn makes a charming knitting basket. Use round toothpicks with tiny beads on the ends for the needles. Split the wool to keep the balls of yarn in scale.

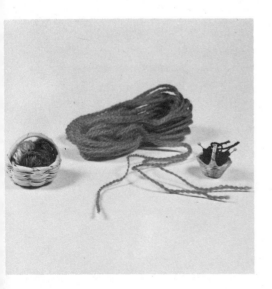

ANIMALS

A tiny china kitten tangled up in a ball of yarn excites almost anyone. A small puppy or dog in front of the fireplace is also charming.

PICTURES

Frame pictures of your children and your grandchildren. To make a new photograph look old, dip a piece of cheesecloth into a light pine stain and wipe over the picture. Frame and hang on the wall of your dollhouse. Lockets and small gold frames are an added touch for your desk or tables. Any small picture that is in proper scale can be framed. Small prints are available in craft stores just for this purpose. Antique them the same as for recent photographs. Miniature frames, already finished, are also available, or make your own frames by mitering 1/4" balsa wood strips to fit the picture. Finish the frame by staining the wood or painting it gold. Glue embossed gold papers to the raw wood frame and paint it gold for yet another look.

FIREPLACE ACCESSORIES

Finish all pieces with a coat of gold paint to look like brass or black paint to look like wrought iron.

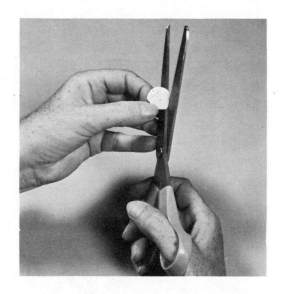

VALANCES

Straight valances can be covered in material to match your decor or
painted and stained to match the woodwork.

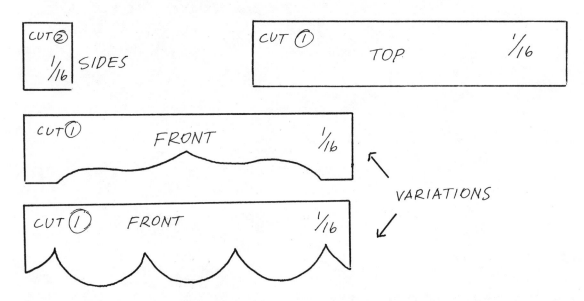

Glue the valance to the wall after you have hung your curtains or drapes.
An added variation is to stencil a pattern on the valance and paint it to
match or coordinate with your decor.

Samples of furniture and china decorations:

Part IV

21 DESIGN IDEAS

Any modest dollhouse can be enhanced by adding shingles and clapboards. Think what the same treatment could do to a two- or three-story dollhouse.

Beauty in simple utilitarian objects characterizes Shaker design. The wall pegs
are a trademark in Shaker homes.

Colonial Williamsburg miniature room.

The clock strikes one, and down comes the mouse.

Miniature 3" x 5" Christmas room.

Curio cabinet to display a small collection.

Brandy snifter and candles form a centerpiece.

Dollhouse Christmas tree (5") is decorated with tiny red and white gingham bows, tiny red berries, and a gold star from an old piece of jewelry.

Glass dome can be used to display one or two special miniatures.

Hand-painted doll furniture was very popular in Europe. Many of the German miniatures are finished in this way. The Pennsylvania Dutch designs used in this country can be traced back to original German and Dutch antiques. (Courtesy of Toys Fantastique, Lake Buena Vista Communities, Inc., a subsidiary of Walt Disney Productions, Lake Buena Vista, Florida.)

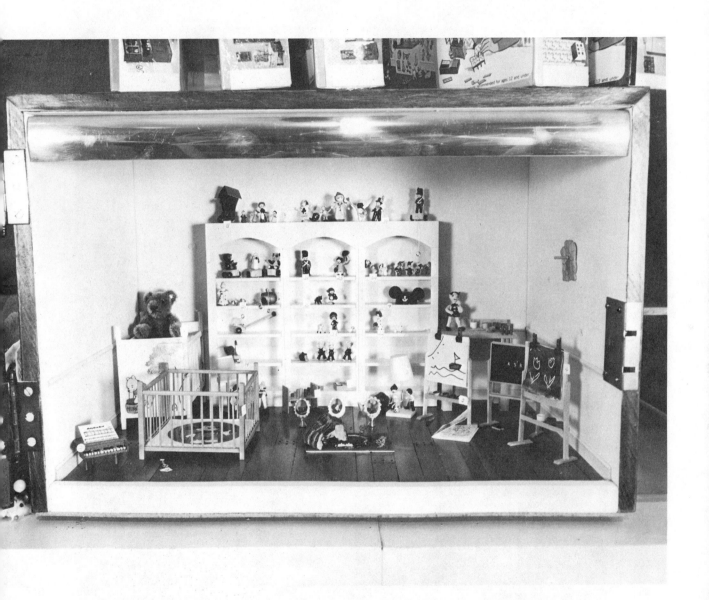

Furniture, toys, and Walt Disney characters for a dollhouse. (Courtesy of Toys Fantastique, Lake Buena Vista Communities, Inc., a subsidiary of Walt Disney Productions, Lake Buena Vista, Florida.)

Thirteen-room Victorian-mansion dollhouse. (Courtesy of Toys Fantastique, Lake Buena Vista Communities, Inc., a subsidiary of Walt Disney Productions, Lake Buena Vista, Florida.)

Interior of the Victorian mansion. (Courtesy of Toys Fantastique, Lake Buena Vista Communities, Inc., a subsidiary of Walt Disney Productions, Lake Buena Vista, Florida.)

Interior of the Victorian mansion. (Courtesy of Toys Fantastique, Lake Buena Vista Communities, Inc., a subsidiary of Walt Disney Productions, Lake Buena Vista, Florida.)

A beautiful replica of a greenhouse in miniature. The gardening tools and plants are in perfect scale. (Courtesy of Toys Fantastique, Lake Buena Vista Communities, Inc., a subsidiary of Walt Disney Productions, Lake Buena Vista, Florida.)